HOLBEIN AND HENRY VIII

STUDIES IN BRITISH ART

UP 3883

HOLBEIN
AND HENRY VIII

ROY STRONG

The Paul Mellon Foundation for British Art
London Routledge & Kegan Paul

First published in Great Britain 1967

By The Paul Mellon Foundation for British Art,
38 Bury Street, London, S.W.1 in association with Routledge
& Kegan Paul Ltd., Broadway House, Carter Lane, London, E.C.4

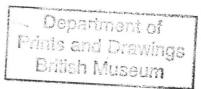

Library of Congress catalogue card no. 67–16160
Printed in Great Britain by Westerham Press, Westerham, Kent
Designed in the offices of The Paul Mellon
Foundation for British Art

TO FRANCES A. YATES

PLATES

Abbreviations in the text

P.R.O.   Public Record Office
B.M.   British Museum
S.P.   State Papers

PREFACE

This book began as a lecture given at the Frick Collection, New York and the National Gallery, Washington in the spring of 1965. It attempts, through the re-creation of Holbein's lost masterpiece, the fresco in the Privy Chamber at Whitehall Palace, to reinterpret the last decade of the artist's life. These years were ones when England lived through the greatest politico-religious upheaval since the Norman Conquest and Holbein's art is one aspect of this shattering crisis. Studies in early Tudor history have undergone a revolution in recent years, in particular through the work of G. R. Elton, but art historians seem to have made little or no attempt to relate the results of these findings to the art of the period. As a past student of the Warburg Institute it gives me great pleasure to take up a theme already touched upon by Fritz Saxl in his lecture 'Holbein and the Reformation'. Saxl saw that the advent of the Reformation was crucial to the understanding of Holbein's earlier work abroad; it is equally crucial to the understanding of his last years in England. Holbein's art becomes one facet of a whole complex of literary and artistic forms used to bolster up the Crown into its new omnipotent position as arbiter of Church as well as State.

It is impossible to list here all the friends and colleagues that I have bored by obstinately talking Holbein but I would like to mention some. David Piper began work on the Chatsworth Cartoon many years ago and generously made over his abandoned notes. Others who have read and criticised the typescript or helped over particular problems include Oliver Millar, E. H. Ramsden, Margot Eates (who produced a splendid new translation of the Latin poem on the Leemput copy), Ronald Lightbown (vital information on the dating of a Latin verse), Hugh Tait, Colin Sorensen (for drawing a reconstruction of the Privy Chamber), John Cornforth, Sir John Summerson, Martin Biddle (the last two on architectural problems concerned with Whitehall), Sir Anthony Blunt (help in the interpretation of a French visitor's description of the wall painting) and Michael Borrie.

I would like to express my gratitude to the Mellon Foundation and its Director, Basil Taylor, both for supporting my researches and for the care and patience lavished on the preparation of this publication by its staff.

Roy Strong
National Portrait Gallery
June 11, 1966

ACKNOWLEDGEMENTS

The following have kindly given permission for works in their possession to be reproduced

Ashmolean Museum, Oxford 17; Bibliothèque Nationale, Paris 53; The Lord Egremont, Frontispiece, 26; Fitzwilliam Museum, Cambridge 46; Frick Collection, New York 7; King's College, Cambridge 23, 42; Kunsthistoriches Museum, Vienna 29; Mauritshuis, The Hague 30; Metropolitan Museum of Art, New York 40; National Gallery, London 37, 45; National Gallery of Art, Washington 15; National Portrait Gallery, London 1, 28; Public Records Office 50 (ii); Royal College of Surgeons 34; Staatliche Museen, Berlin 6; Thyssen-Bornemisza Collection 32; Walker Art Gallery, Liverpool 38; Worshipful Company of Barbers 54

Photographic Acknowledgements

Alinari/Mansell Collection 36; Ashmolean Museum, Oxford 17; Bibliothèque Nationale, Paris 53; British Museum 5, 8, 10, 41; A. C. Cooper Ltd 3, 4, 20, 21, 22, 25, 39; Courtauld Institute of Art 26, 34, 54; A. Dingjan, The Hague 30; John R. Freeman & Co 9, 49; Frick Art Collection 7; Kunsthistoriches Museum, Vienna 29; Metropolitan Museum of Art, New York 40; Ministry of Public Building and Works 47; National Gallery, London 32, 37, 45; National Gallery of Art, Washington 15; National Portrait Gallery, London 1, 27, 28, 33, 43; G. Spearman, Windsor 31; Staatliche Museen, Berlin 6; Stearn & Sons 46; Walker Art Gallery, Liverpool 38; Warburg Institute 48, 51

THAT RARE PIECE

' . . . it is a dismal sight to behold such a glorious, famous, and much renowned palace reduced to a heap of rubbish and ashes, which the day before might justly contend with any palace in the world for riches, nobility, honour and grandeur'[1]

[1] *Account of Fire*, Wren Society, VII, 1930, p80.

Plate 1 Hans Holbein
Cartoon for the Privy Chamber Wall-painting
Infra-red photograph 101½ × 54 inches
National Portrait Gallery, London

On the afternoon of January 4th, 1698, a Dutch maidservant was busy drying linen in the upper room of a gentleman's lodgings at Whitehall.[1] A charcoal fire had been lit to facilitate her task, and the linen hung round it unattended. In a few hours 'merciless and devouring flames' swept through the ancient palace of the Tudor and Stuart sovereigns. Neither the rushed appearance of fire engines, nor the blowing up of parts of the palace, did anything to impede its spectacular progress. The fire raged on through the night destroying not only a hundred and fifty houses, residences and lodgings of the nobility, but the great state apartments of the King. When finally it was extinguished at about eight o'clock the next morning, those who came to view the still smoking ruins saw little but a charred wilderness, acres of blackened brick and twisted iron where once there had been one of the most famous and legendary of Tudor royal palaces. Admittedly, Inigo Jones' banqueting house still stood – blackened and begrimed – as did the so-called Holbein and King Street gateways, but between King Street and the waterside the palace had vanished. John Evelyn summed up the whole day's events with characteristic epigrammatic concision: 'White-hall utterly burnt to the ground, nothing but the walls & ruines left'.[2]

Those, that wintery morning, who penetrated further and stumbled their way through the rubble of the palace towards the brickwork shell of the old state rooms could have cast their eyes upwards to catch a glimpse of a famous wall painting. On the walls of the Privy Chamber there could still be seen the remnants of Hans Holbein the Younger's masterpiece, his monumental apotheosis of the Tudor dynasty. It had survived earlier hazards reasonably unimpaired. Evelyn had visited the palace forty years before under the Commonwealth expecting to discover it desecrated by the regicides, but 'was glad to find, they had not much defac'd that rare piece',[3] and it had survived Wren's rebuilding of the privy lodgings in 1685[4] and an earlier fire in 1691.[5] Even after the ultimate disaster of 1698 an effort was made to move the part of the wall on which the fresco was painted, 'but all proved ineffectual'.[6]

All that we know now of 'that rare piece' is contained in two copies on canvas condensing into inches the contents of so many feet [Plate 2]. Remigius van Leemput's copies, one commissioned by Charles II in 1667, withhold as much as they communicate. Only the miraculous survival of part of the original drawing, the famous Chatsworth Cartoon now in the National Portrait Gallery [Plate 1], remains to convey to posterity something of the compelling magic it was capable of evoking. It is almost as though we had a paper cartoon for the left hand part of Raphael's *Parnassus* together with a mid-seventeenth century copy

1 On the burning of Whitehall see P.R.O.S.P. 32/9.f.9.; B.M. Additional MS 32504 f. 54.

2 *The Diary of John Evelyn*, ed. E.S. de Beer, Oxford, 1955, V, p283.

3 Ibid., III, p166.

4 Wren Society, op. cit, p75.

5 Evelyn, *Diary*, ed cit, V, p47: 'a suddaine & terible Fire burnt downe all the buildings over the stone Gallery'.

6 H. Buckeridge, *An Essay towards an English School of Painting*, in De Piles, *The Art of Painting*, English ed, 3rd ed, n.d., p387.

of the fresco and were faced with the task of re-creating from these fragments, plus a handful of written documents, the whole of the first of the Vatican stanze. In this instance, it is Whitehall in its brief glittering heyday that needs to be relived in the mind's eye. What was this room called the Privy Chamber, and who are these sumptuously clad people and why are they standing grouped around an enormous stone altar bearing an inscription in Latin hexameters?

The figure that dominates the scene, legs astride like some latter-day colossus, is the King. Henry VIII is our touchstone. Holbein's painting is one facet of the most lavish and intensive patronage of the visual arts by the Crown prior to the accession of Charles I. It is an expression at once of the King's 'magnificence' and of his political power. A small army of painters, sculptors, architects and craftsmen were employed throughout the 1530's to manifest in terms of paint, stone, wood, metal, glass and fabric the hard facts of a political and religious revolution. It is in this light that we must reconsider Holbein's art for he, like them, was concerned with glorifying a man who embodied supreme power, not only in the state but in the church, and upon whose brow now sat an 'imperial crown'.

Plate 2   George Vertue after Remegius van Leemput
Privy Chamber Wall-painting
Engraving

THE IMPERIAL CROWN

'*And in that place he hathe set princes, whom, as representours of his Image unto men, he wolde have to be reputed in the supreme and most highe rowme and to excelle amonge all other humayne creatures . . .*'

Stephen Gardiner, *De Vera Obedientia*[1]

[1]Stephen Gardiner, *Obedience in Church and State*, ed. P. Janelle, Cambridge, 1930, p89.

No other act had more far-reaching effects on the concept of the English Crown than the one passed by the Reformation Parliament early in 1533, the famous Act in Restraint of Appeals. Its preamble was to affect the whole Tudor myth and is so important that it must be quoted in full.

'Where by divers sundry old authentic histories and chronicles it is manifestly declared and expressed that this realm of England is an empire, and so hath been accepted in the world, governed by one supreme head and king having the dignity and royal estate of the imperial crown of the same, unto whom a body politic, compact of all sorts and degrees of people divided in terms and by names of spiritualty and temporalty, be bounden and owe next to God a natural and humble obedience . . .'.[1]

This Act, carefully guided through, and in many parts directly phrased, by Henry's minister, Thomas Cromwell,[2] becomes the bulwark of the myth of Empire which is crucial for the understanding of the imagery surrounding the Monarchy in the post-Reformation period. Over the coming centuries it was to have a profound influence not only on politico-religious ideas but on the whole mythology of Monarchy as it expressed itself in public buildings, painting, poetry and pageantry. All the arts in service of the Monarchy were conditioned by this fundamental concept of 'the imperial crown'.[3]

The imperialism of the 1530's was of a vigorous, offensive kind and it would be as well to remind ourselves, briefly, of the powers which the Crown had assumed to itself. In 1531, Henry had been accorded the title of 'singular protector, only and supreme lord, and, as far as the law of Christ allows, even Supreme Head'. The year after followed the Submission of the Clergy, and in 1533 the Act in Restraint of Appeals which finally broke with Rome and contained in its preamble the classic exposition of the 'Imperial' status enjoyed by the Kings of England. Finally, in 1534, the Supremacy Act put on the Statute Book the King's claim to dominance over the affairs of the Church of England: 'the King our Sovereign Lord, his heirs and successors Kings of this realm, shall be taken, accepted, and reputed the only Supreme Head in earth of the Church of England, called *Anglicana Ecclesia*'.[4] Henry now exercised in his own right the *potestas jurisdictionis* over the temporal affairs of the Church and also, at least in some degree, the *potestas ordinis*. In the latter he did not of course perform the duties of a priest but could and did by royal prerogative determine doctrine and ritual. In this way through a series of statutes spanning the years 1534 to 1545 the English Crown absorbed the entire legislative, judicial, administrative, financial and even doctrinal prerogatives of the Church. By the very close of the reign Henry had the right to make doctrinal decrees by letters patent.

Simultaneously with the passing of the Act in Restraint of Appeals with its assertions concerning 'the imperial Crown of this Realm' comes the publication of Polydore Vergil's *Anglica Historia*.[5] Although this Italian humanist, an exile from the Montefeltre court at Urbino, had completed his great work in 1513 it was not published until twenty years later. In 1533 Cromwell and the King saw this book as a means to justify the imperial status claimed by the Crown, a compendium as it were of the 'divers sundry old authentic histories and chronicles' to which the crucial Act referred as evidence. The book indeed was brought up to date with a special emphasis on 'the imperial theme'. Vergil, a man trained among the Latinists of the papal chancery, made free use of the word *imperium* in the humanist sense of meaning any unit of dominion that had come to greatness through force but whatever he may strictly have meant by his use of the *imperium* it was inevitable that it brought in its

1 G. R. Elton, *The Tudor Constitution*, Cambridge, 1960, p344.

2 See G. R. Elton, *The Evolution of a Reformation Statute*, English Historical Review, LXIV, 1949, pp174-97.

3 On Tudor and more particularly Elizabethan imperialism see F. A. Yates, *Queen Elizabeth as Astraea*, Journal of the Warburg and Courtauld Institutes, X, 1947, esp. pp37-56, the same author's *Charles V et l'idée d'Empire*, in Les Fêtes de Charles V in Les Fêtes de la Renaissance, ed. J. Jaquot, Paris, 1960, II, pp57-97. See also G. R. Elton, *England under the Tudors* London, 1955, pp160-62.

4 G. R. Elton, *Tudor Constitution*, op. cit, p355.

5 See R. Koebner, *The Imperial Crown of this Realm*, Bulletin of the Institute of Historical Research, XXVI, 1953, pp29-52. *The Anglica Historia of Polydore Vergil*, ed. D. Hay, Camden Society, LXXIV, 1950.

train a whole complex of other ideas. The climax of his saga was the reign of Constantine from whose sacred person the *imperium* descended as of right to the Kings of England: *Quamquam postea haud perdiu in Constantini dono imperium mansit . . . tamen decus ipsius imperii non potuit cadere, cum etiam nunc reges Angliae more maiorum, diademate imperiali utantur, ut munere ab Imperatore Constantino in suos posteros collato.*[1] The position of Constantine was seen as crucial evidence for the English assertion of the position claimed by the jurists of Philip the Fair, that every king *est in patria sua imperator*. Above all, the arguments clinched Henry's claim to dominance in the ecclesiastical sphere for Constantine had borne equal sway over both. Attempts were made to prove that the original traditions of the *Ecclesia Anglicana* were identical with the fundamental principles which prevailed at the time of Constantine. Nor was such material scorned as a weapon in diplomacy. 'The King', explained the Duke of Norfolk to the amazed imperial ambassador, Chapuys, 'had a right of empire in his kingdom, and recognised no superior; that there had been an English man who had conquered Rome, to wit, Brennus, Constantine had reigned here and the mother of Constantine was English'.[2] Chapuys, entirely unaware of the historical traditions that could produce such extraordinary arguments and himself a representative of the reigning Holy Roman Emperor, dismissed such spurious claims as absurd and irrelevant.

But behind the convolutions of policy out of which emerged the Anglican Church in the 16th century glittered this vision of a primitive church, pure of doctrine and as yet untarnished with papal corruptions, governed peacefully by a great emperor. Savage and arbitary though the King may seem in retrospect, to those who believed and built up the royal myth he embodied a return of Church and State to the ancient purity of his great ancestor. Henry VIII would wish to be seen in the words of his Archbishop of Canterbury, Thomas Cranmer, describing the golden age of Constantine:

'When Constantine was christened, then was true religion first set forth and openly preached by public authority . . . In this prince's time, and by his authority, was kept the first and best general council of Nice, where was set forth our common creed, containing shortly the chief and most necessary articles of our belief'.[3]

These writings, in which the powers of the English Monarchy were radically rethought and redefined, had a fundamental influence on the imagery surrounding the Crown for over three hundred years. In the case of Henry VIII it is not the exact politico-religious consequences which need affect us but the actual idea of Monarchy as it was hammered by the propagandists in the employ of Thomas Cromwell and reflected in contemporary eulogies of the King. The thought context of Holbein's definitive image of Henry VIII is not that of the Shakespeare play but of the political pamphleteers and reforming theologians of the thirties, the Novus Constantinus who, having thrown out the Pope and his corruptions, ushers in a new era of 'imperial' purity.

The new theories of Monarchy were expounded by means of what was the earliest deliberate propaganda programme, in the modern sense of the word, in English history.[4] Writers including John Rastell, Thomas Starkey and Richard Morison were employed by Thomas Cromwell to defend the powers of the crown in things ecclesiastical and to denounce those who dared raise voice in opposition. The campaign did not only embody a literary offensive, it also took the form of recommending the preaching of sermons against the Pope throughout the country, of exhibiting his vices on every church door and of speaking publicly in

1 Polydore Vergil, *Anglica Historia*, Basle, 1534, p46.

2 Chapuys to Charles V, January 13th, 1531, *Letters and Papers of Henry VIII, 1531-32*, pp19-21.

3 T. Cranmer, *A Confutation of Unwritten Verities* in *Miscellaneous Writings*, Parker Society, 1846, p15

4 The whole campaign is admirably dealt with in W. G. Zeeveld, *Foundations of Tudor Policy*, Harvard U.P., 1958, pp128 ff.: Zeeveld's views on Cromwell are thrown into even greater relief by Elton's reassessment of his place in the revolution of the thirties: see G. R. Elton, *King or Minister?: The Man behind the Henrician Reformation*, History, XXXIX, 1954, pp216-32; *The Political Creed of Thomas Cromwell,*

Transactions of the Royal Historical Society, 5th series, VI, 1956, pp69-92.

1 See J. W. Harris, *John Bale, A Study in the Minor Literature of the Reformation,* Illinois Studies in Language and Literature, XXV, 1940.

2 S. Anglo, *An Early Tudor Programme for Plays and other Demonstrations against the Pope,* Journal of the Warburg and Courtauld Institutes, XX, 1957, pp176-79.

denunciation of him. By the mid-thirties the virulent productions of John Bale and his associates were taking, under Cromwell's patronage, the religious offensive on to the stage.[1] Richard Morison's *A Discourse touching the Reformation of the Lawes of England* sums up the whole campaign in a passage following the recommendation to the King of an annual antipapal festival to be celebrated all over the country in place of the old superstitious holy days. He writes that the Robin Hood plays:

'. . . shulde be forbodden and deleted and others devysed to set forthe and declare lyvely before the people eies the abhomynation and wickednes of the bisshop of Rome, monkes, ffreers, nonnes, and suche like, and to declare and open to them thobedience that your subiectes by goddes and mans lawes owe unto your magestie. Into the commen people thynges sooner enter by the eies, then by the eares: remembryng more better that they see then that they heere . . .'.[2]

This attitude, which has long been recognised as being crucial to the understanding of the political, religious and literary history of the period, has never been applied to its artistic policies. These too must be viewed as part of the tissue of ideas being woven around the Monarchy in the fifteen thirties. We only have to glance at the portrait of Henry VIII at Hampton Court holding up the scroll inscribed *Go ye into all the world, and preach the gospel to every creature* [Plate 3] to recognise the immediate impact of the Reformation on the arts.

Plate 3   Attributed to Joos van Cleve *Henry VIII*
28 × 22 inches   Reproduced by gracious permission of
Her Majesty the Queen

The whole fabric of the artistic policy of the Crown during the 1530's is woven around a never-ending theme of the triumph of the King over the Pope, of the crown over the tiara. Anti-papal paintings[1] for instance, found honoured places on the walls of the royal palaces; examples are recorded in an inventory of 1542: 'oone table of the naked truth with the works of the busshop of Rome set fourth in it', a second of 'the picture of the king his highness standing upon a miter with iij Crownes (i.e. the papal tiara) having a serpent with vij hedds going owt of it having a sworde in his hand wherein is written Verbum Dei' and 'a table of the busshope of Rome and the four Evangelists casting stones upon him'.[2] One was an allegory based on the old theme of *Veritas Temporis Filia*, Truth the Daughter of Time, bringing to light the iniquities of the Pope;[3] the second the King vanquishing the Pope identified as the beast of the Apocalypse, by issuing the English bible, a picture perhaps identical with one destroyed in Mary's reign: 'The phismanye of King Henry the eight painted in a table, like an antique, annotated 'broken because it was the destruction of the Bishop of Rome'.[4] The third still survives at Hampton Court [Plate 4]. In this the true light of the Gospel – the candle hovering over the distant city – triumphs over the falsehood of Rome and the four Evangelists lay low the Pope and his accomplices, Hypocrisy and Avarice. A rosary, a holy water stoop, a cardinal's hat and papal indulgences litter the ground beneath the sprawling pontiff. The artist is Girolamo da Treviso, a Florentine, who, like Holbein found service with Henry VIII.[5] An important connexion exists also between this picture and a woodcut illustration for the 1536 translation of the Bible into English [Plate 5]. The woodcut, which is an illustration to the third book of Moses appears to have been the basis for the picture and in addition provides a final nuance to its meaning for it alludes to the Pope as the blasphemous man: 'And the Lord spake unto Moses, and said: Bring him that cursed out of the host, and let all them that hear it, lay their hands upon his head, and let the whole congregation stone him'.

1 Anti-papal paintings as part of the English Reformation propaganda go back to at least 1527. In that year Sir Thomas Wyat, on his return from Rome, had composed a device depicting the pope as the Minotaur, 'a triple crown on his head, both as it were falling', in the midst of a maze, a ball of thread at the top with broken chains and the legend: *Laqueus contritus est et nos liberati sumus*. The King took much pleasure 'to hear discourse of it at my lord's return'. See M. Conway, *Portraits of the Wyat Family*, Burlington Magazine, XVI, 1910, pp154-59.

2 *Three Inventories of the year 1542, 1547 and 1549-50 of Pictures in the Collection of Henry VIII and Edward VI*, ed. W. A. Shaw, Courtauld Institute of Art Text for the Study of Art History, I, 1937, pp30, 35, 56.

3 On which see F. Saxl, 'Veritas Filia Temporis' in *Philosophy and History*, Essays presented to E. Cassirer, ed. R. Klibansky and H. J. Paton, Oxford, 1936, pp202-10.

4 *Historical MSS. Comm.*, Hatfield, I.p130. On a later anti-papal painting see Roy Strong, *Edward VI and the Pope: A Tudor anti-papal allegory and its setting*, Journal of the Warburg and Courtauld Institute, XXIII, 1960, pp311-13.

5 On which see P. Pouncey, *Girolamo da Treviso in the service of Henry VIII*, Burlington Magazine, XCV, 1953, pp208-11.

Plate 4   Girolamo da Treviso *The Four Evangelists stoning the Pope*
27 × 33 inches   Reproduced by gracious permission of
Her Majesty the Queen

Plate 5   Artist unknown *The stoning of the Blasphemous Man*
Woodcut
From the 1536 translation of the Bible

1 On the Crown's building policy, see J. Summerson, *Architecture in Britain, 1530-1830*, London, 1963, revised and enlarged ed, pp1-11. This outline will be greatly supplemented when the relevant volume in the history of the King's Works appears by Martin Biddle.

2 On the importance of these temporary miseen-scéne see S. Anglo, *Le Camp de Drap d'Or et les entreveues d'Henri VIII et Charles V* in Les Fetes de Charles V in Les Fêtes de la Renaissance, ed, J. Jaquot, Paris, 1960, II, pp115-18, 127-32; and *La Salle de Banquet et le Théatre construits à Greenwich pour les Fêtes Franco-Anglaises de 1527* in Le lieu théatral à la Renaissance, ed, J. Jaquot, Paris, 1964, pp274-88. The former deals with the temporary palace at Guisnes of 1520 for the Field of Cloth of Gold and the latter with that of 1527 for which Holbein seems to have been the central figure working under the guidance of the King's astronomer, Nicholas Kratzer. If this had taken permanent form it would, perhaps, have offered a parallel to Raphael's astrological ceiling in the Farnese Palace. The décor was clearly à l'antique.

3 On Nonsuch see J. Dent, *The Quest for Nonsuch*, London, 1962.

4 Ibid, pp96-98.

5 S. Gardiner, *Obedience in Church and State*, p96–97.

The image of the Crown was also immensely enhanced by the launching of a major building programme.[1] Up until the close of the twenties, Richmond and Greenwich had been the main royal residences with Bridewell as a London palace. Then quite suddenly the tide turns with Wolsey's fall from power. In 1525 he presented Henry with Hampton Court and five years later York Place was taken over. Both these were transformed into royal palaces with elaborate and extensive additions. Building went on at almost breakneck speed throughout the thirties at York Place (soon to be Whitehall), Hampton Court and St James's, while other work progressed in addition at Bridewell, New Hall, Oatlands and Hunsdon. Finally, in 1538, came Nonsuch. The importance of Henry VIII's schemes is very evident when it is realised that his palaces remained for nearly two hundred years the acknowledged residences of the English Crown. The effect on the general public of these magnificent settings must have been considerable and the gasping admiration the interiors (not, however, the exteriors) evoked from foreigners throughout the century is testament to their success. These palaces and their décors were realisations in brick, stone, wood and plaster of the glittering ephemeral settings devised for court festivals, such as the Field of Cloth of Gold.[2] Now, thanks to the vast influx of ecclesiastical wealth, they took on permanent form.

Whitehall will be examined in detail shortly, but as an instance of Henry's policy we might cast an eye towards one of the most perfect expositions of the new monarchical ideas, the palace of Nonsuch.[3] The village of Cudlington was razed to the ground to make way for this building which began to arise at almost frantic speed at the hands of a whole army of workmen from April 1538 onwards. All contemporary visitors to the palace were overcome by its wonders and its two most prominent features were its great octagonal towers and its *a l'antique* plasterwork. Directly inspired by the work at Fontainebleau for Francis I and carried out under the supervision of one of his masterworkmen, Nicolò da Modena, hundreds of feet of wallspace were encrusted with plasterwork panels in high relief. These found a focal point in the inner court which clearly was governed by a carefully conceived iconographic scheme, of which we know only fragments. As the visitor passed into the inner courtyard through a gateway crowned with statues of Roman Emperors, with their imperial implications, he was confronted with a statue of Henry VIII enthroned trampling under foot a lion, flanked on either side by bands of plasterwork panels depicting the arts and virtues, the labours of Hercules and classical gods and goddesses. The Elizabethan chronicler of the Nonsuch marvels provides a succinct and admirable analysis of the general intentions of this astounding display. 'Can harm befall', he writes, 'the body politic when its most sagacious king wielding the sceptre is protected, on the right, by the arts and virtues and avenging goddesses, on the left by the feats of Hercules and the tender care of the gods'.[4] It was, as Lord Protector Cromwell's surveyor noted a century later, a 'very fair and curious structure', It was, in its heyday, a fitting setting for a King who claimed to be 'in this world present the person of God'.[5]

THE KING'S PAINTER

' Mr. Hans, the royal painter, the Apelles of our time.'

Nicholas Bourbon to Thomas Solimar[1]

[1] A. Woltmann, *Holbein and his Time*, trans., F. E. Bunnett, London, 1872, p369.

Plate 6   Hans Holbein *Pageant Arch for Anne Boleyn's entry into London*
$16\frac{5}{8} \times 15\frac{1}{8}$ inches Staatliche Museen, Berlin

It is against this sustained campaign of propaganda on behalf of the new concepts of Monarchy that Holbein's second visit must be viewed.[1] He becomes drawn into the orbit of those who were creating a new myth of Monarchy. Not enough emphasis can be given to this drastic change of milieu so different from that of his first visit in 1527, when he moved in the tranquil, pious humanist circle of Sir Thomas More and his friends. In 1529 Holbein himself had declared his allegiance to the reform by refusing to take communion until the exact nature of the sacrament were further explained to him.[2] Three years later he reappears in England, finding his patrons amongst the merchants of the German Steelyard for whom he painted portraits and the great wall decorations of the Triumphs of Riches and Poverty. Then suddenly, in 1537, come the payments in the royal accounts and Holbein takes up his position as King's Painter until his death in 1543.

Holbein's return to England coincides with the years of revolution and opens with the complete collapse of the circle from which, during his first visit, he had received patronage: Archbishop Warham died in 1532 to make way for Thomas Cranmer, and Sir Thomas More went to the Tower in 1534 to be executed the year after. Holbein's close connexion with this circle may well account for the non-materialisation of royal patronage during the very years when on Whitehall Palace alone a small army of painters was working. The lack may also be explained by the pageant arch he designed for the Merchants of the Steelyard in honour of Anne Boleyn's entry into London as Queen in May 1533. This depicted Apollo and the Muses but, alas, also displayed the imperial eagle [Plate 6]. Read as an allusion to the nephew and advocate of the divorced Queen Catherine, the Emperor Charles V, this was all too ill-received by the court who saw in it a calculated insult to the new Queen.[3]

1 The known historical facts used here concerning Holbein's second English visit have remained practically unchanged since the close of the 19th century. They are included in all the standard works on Holbein: R. N. Wornum, *Some Account of the Life and Works of Hans Holbein*, London, 1867; A. Woltmann, op. cit; A. Chamberlain, *Hans Holbein the Younger*, London, 1913, 2 vols; H. A. Schmidt, *Hans Holbein der Jüngere*, Basle, 1948, 3 vols., P. Ganz, *The Paintings of Hans Holbein*, London, 1950 contains historical data.

2 The early relationship between Holbein and the Reformation is discussed by F. Saxl, *Holbein and the Reformation*, in Lectures, London, 1957, I, pp277-85. Saxl does not take the story on to include Holbein's second English visit.

3 A. Chamberlain, *Holbein*, II, p32.

Plate 7   Hans Holbein *Thomas Cromwell*
$30\frac{7}{8} \times 25\frac{3}{8}$ inches
The Frick Collection, New York

1 P. Ganz, *Holbein*, pp.86, 133; Chamberlain, *Holbein*, II, pp10-11, 58.

2 A. Chamberlain, *Holbein*, II, p232.

Evidence would suggest that Holbein's potentialities were recognised by the man who directed the propaganda programme of the 1530's, Thomas Cromwell. The links between Holbein and the Cromwell circle are strong and altogether convincing. Two men, John Godsalve of Norwich and John of Antwerp, both active in Cromwell's service, knew him.[1] Sometime about 1534, Thomas Cromwell himself sat in his capacity as Master of the Jewel House [Plate 7], and in 1538 Holbein actually appears in the Cromwell accounts.[2] In 1536 Holbein's woodcut frontispiece adorns the title page to that landmark of the English Reformation, Coverdale's translation of the Bible into English, a publication brought out under Cromwell's guidance and patronage. Three years later Holbein presents to the King, as a New Year's gift, a portrait of the baby Prince Edward inscribed with Latin verses by Richard Morison, Cromwell's master pamphleteer. This sequence of events and connexions is irresistible and undeniable: the link between Holbein, master artist and craftsman, and Cromwell, master propagandist and politician, is assured.

Holbein's value as an accurate recorder of the King's brides, actual and potential, is too well known and well documented to need repetition here. Nor is this the place to discuss his impact on the decorative arts, embodied in an abundance of ravishing designs for plate, jewellery and other costly articles for the consumption of the court. The drawings for these, which need re-studying in detail, present many problems, not the least of which being that it is clear that some must be the work of other artists. Instead we shall follow the thread that will lead us to a contemplation of Holbein's supreme contribution to the vision of Monarchy as envisaged by his patron, Cromwell, the group portrait of Henry VIII and his family in the Privy Chamber at Whitehall.

There are three main groups of work executed either during or just after his painting of the great fresco which belong to the fabric of the story. They are the frontispiece to the English translation of the Bible, a group of anti-clerical woodcuts, and his portrait of Edward VI in the National Gallery, Washington. All three are demonstrations of the belief – like that which governed the wall painting – that 'things sooner enter by the eyes, than by the ears, remembering more better that they see than that they hear'.

On the Bible frontispiece [Plate 8] Holbein creates an image which was to be a definitive one for the Tudor and Stuart Kings, that of the Monarch enthroned clasping the sword of justice and issuing the English Bible, a variant iconographically of the classic renaissance emblematic device *Ex utroque Caesar* [Plate 9], the Emperor bearing the sword and book, allusions to the duality of his triumphs in peace as well as war.[3] The image of the King as the purveyor to his people of the Word of God can be traced down through representations of Edward VI [Plate 10] and Elizabeth I [Plate 11] on into the Stuart period. As it appeared in varying forms on successive editions and translations of the Bible, laid down by Act of Parliament to be in every parish Church, this image of the Monarchy must have been familiar to everyone who lived in the England of the Tudors and Stuarts.

3 E.g. P. Giovio and G. Siymeoni, *Le Sententiose Imprese*, Lyons, 1561, p10.

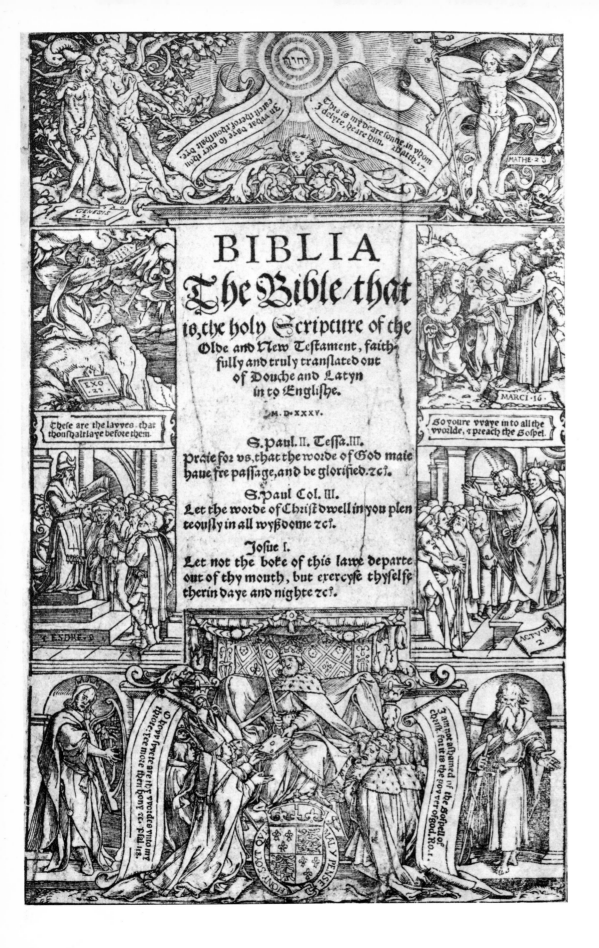

Plate 9   Artist unknown
The Emperor bearing the book and sword
Wood engraving

Plate 8   Hans Holbein
Title page to the 1536 translation of the Bible
Wood engraving

Plate 10   Artist unknown *Edward VI with the sword and Bible*
Woodcut from Thomas Cranmer's *Catechism* 1548

Plate 11   Crispin van de Passe I
Queen Elizabeth I with the sword and Bible   Engraving

The iconography of the title page, with its stress on the preaching of the Word, is overtly reformist, and the keys entrusted by Christ to Peter alone, the interpretation upon which the Popes based their claim to primacy, are here clasped by every apostle as equals. The dedication reflects that this is the year after the Act of Supremacy, for Kings are hailed as 'in this world present, the person of God . . . he only under God is the Chief head of all the congregation and church of the same'. The King is surrounded by archetypes of himself. In the dedication he is directly referred to as Moses, who appears top left, receiving the tables of law, and thanked for bringing his subjects out of 'the cruel hands of our spiritual Pharoa', the Roman pontiff. He is also hailed as David, who stands to the bottom left with his harp, for the King of England is another David who has subdued the monster Goliath of the Antichrist of Rome. Flanked by David and St Paul, Henry is seen as embodying the virtues of the Old Testament Kings and the missionary zeal of the apostles.

Three small woodcut designs are more overtly anti-clerical. They take up and re-state, in more savage and overt form, Holbein's earlier marginal sketches in Erasmus's *Praise of Folly*. None of the woodcuts appeared during Holbein's lifetime, all appearing in 1548 as illustrations to Cranmer's *Catechism* and to Urbanus Regius' *Lytle Treatise*. All depict New Testament scenes in which the scribes and pharisees are shown dressed as monks and clergy. In one the hireling shepherd, a monk, flees from his flock leaving it to the ravening wolf

[Plate 12]. A lecture on prayer in Cranmer's *Catechism* is accompanied by a woodcut of the parable of the pharisee and the publican: the self-righteous pharisee who casts his eyes proudly heavenwards is again attired in monastic garb [Plate 13]. The commentary on the Lord's Prayer contains a final woodcut to accompany the phrase 'But deliver us from evil', which depicts Christ casting out the devil, the pharisees attired once more in clerical and monastic guise [Plate 14]. Published long after the Dissolution of the Monasteries, the last of which were dissolved in 1539, they were quite irrelevant to the religious situation in the early years of Edward's reign. Holbein must have designed these woodcuts for publication in connexion with the attack on the monastic orders which reached its height in 1536, with the suppression of the lesser houses, and ended with the final, total suppression, three years later. Either some violently anti-clerical book was published and no copy survives, or it was planned and abandoned, the blocks remaining to be used in later publications. They remain as fragments suggesting an incipient visual campaign in denunciation of the Pope and his adherents at once more subtle and insidious than the violence and crudity we associate with Lutheran woodcut propaganda.

A final direct connexion between Cromwell's pamphleteers and Holbein exists in the portrait of the baby prince Edward VI presented as a New Year's gift to his father on January 1st, 1539 [Plate 15].[1] The Latin verses beneath should be examined in detail for they are by Sir Richard Morison. In translation they read:

'Little one! imitate your father, and be the heir of his virtue, the world contains nothing greater – Heaven and Nature could scarcely give a son whose glory should surpass that of such a father. You only equal the acts of your parent, the wishes of men cannot go beyond this. Surpass him, and you have surpassed all the kings the world ever worshipped, and none will ever surpass you'.[2]

Even though Holbein succeeds in instilling into this portrait something of the joyous irreverence of childhood the verses usher us back into the world of Reformation propaganda.[3]

Plate 12   Designed by Hans Holbein
The hireling shepherd
Woodcut from Urbanus Regius
Lytle Treatise 1548

1 A. Chamberlain, *Holbein*, II, p164.

2 The translation is taken from R. N. Wornum, *Holbein*, p324 note. The original reads: PARVVLE PATRISSA, PATRIÆ VIRTVTIS ET HÆRES|ESTO, NIHIL MAIVS MAXIMVS ORBIS HABET.|GNATVM VIX POSSVNT CO ELVM ET NATVRA DEDISSE,|HVIVS QVEM PATRIS, VICTVS HONORET HONOS.| ÆQVATO TANTVM, TANTI TV FACTA PARENTIS,|VOTA HOMINVM, VIX QVO PROGREDIANTVR, HABENT|VINCITO, VICISTI QVOT REGES PRISCVS ADORAT| ORBIS NEC TE QVI VINCERE POSSIT, ERIT.

3 On Morison see W. Gordon Zeeveld, *Richard Morison, Public Apologist for Henry VIII*, Publications of the Modern Language Association, LV, 1940, pp406-25; same author's *Foundations of Tudor Policy*, passim.

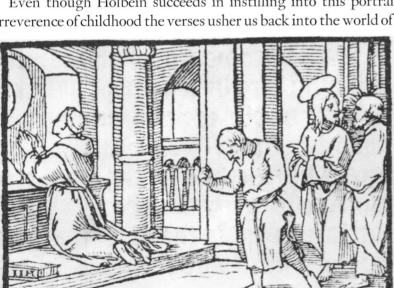

Plate 13   Designed by Hans Holbein
Parable of the Pharisee and the Publican
Woodcut from Thomas Cranmer's *Catechism* 1548

Plate 14   Designed by Hans Holbein
Christ casting out the Devil
Woodcut from Thomas Cranmer's *Catechism* 1548

Their author is a key figure linking Holbein directly into the circle of those who, under the guidance of Thomas Cromwell, were paid apologists for the official policy of the Crown. Between the years 1536 and 1539 Morison was employed to defend the divorce of Catherine of Aragon, to support the Supremacy of the Crown in things ecclesiastical and to denounce the rebels who made up the Pilgrimage of Grace. Holbein should be seen as one of this team of Morison and his companions, as one facet of the whole apparatus which was unloosed around the Crown in the 1530's to create an image potent enough to hold together a people in loyalty to the Crown in the face of a break with the ancient historic claims of a united Christendom.

PARVVLE PATRISSA, PATRIÆ VIRTVTIS ET HÆRES
ESTO, NIHIL MAIVS MAXIMVS ORBIS HABET.
GNATVM VIX POSSVNT COELVM ET NATVRA DEDISSE,
HVIVS QVEM PATRIS, VICTVS HONORET HONOS.
ÆQVATO TANTVM, TANTI TV FACTA PARENTIS,
VOTA HOMINVM, VIX QVO PROGREDIANTVR, HABENT
VINCITO, VICISTI. QVOT REGES PRISCVS ADORAT
ORBIS, NEC TE QVI VINCERE POSSIT, ERIT.

Plate 15   Hans Holbein *Edward VI as Prince of Wales*
22⅜ × 17⅜ inches National Gallery of Art, Washington,
Andrew Mellon Collection

GLORIOUS WHYTE HALL

'. . . the glorious *Whyte hall, a regall mancion scytuate upon the Thamise bewtifull and lardge, adorned with manie fayre galleries, stately furnished with moste artificiall and dilectable pictures, tables, and such like princely ornaments.*'

John Norden, 1592[1]

[1]W. B. Rye, *England as seen by Foreigners in the Days of Queen Elizabeth and James I,* London, 1865, p99.

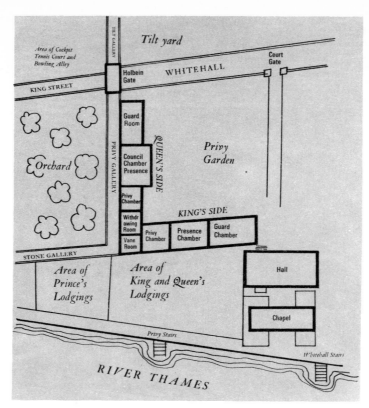

Plate 16   *Diagram of Whitehall Palace in 1537*

Plate 17   Anthonis Wyngaerde *View of Whitehall Palace from the Thames*
Ashmolean Museum, Oxford

Whitehall as it was in 1537 is not easy to reconstruct [Plates 16, 17].[1] The approach to the palace by land from the City was by way of Charing Cross which led into King Street, a highway which ran straight through the palace and its gardens, dividing it into two parts. One ran to the east, consisting of the state apartments and offices and privy garden, down to the water's edge: the others, the pleasure gardens, the tiltyard, bowling alley, tennis court and park, extended to the west. It reflected Bacon's fundamental dictum on palaces: 'You cannot have a perfect palace, except you have two sides, a side for the banquet, as is spoken in the book of Hester; and a side for the household: the one for feasts and triumphs, and the other for dwelling'.[2] To the eyes of visiting foreigners in the 17th century, the outside seemed little more 'than an assemblage of several houses, badly built, at different times',[3] thrown into all too dismal relief by the splendours of Inigo Jones' palladian banqueting house. In 1537, this arbitrary encrustation had not disfigured it. But this impression may indeed reflect the rushed and therefore often shoddy workmanship that is characteristic of Henry VIII's building projects.

York Place had been the London residence of the Archbishops of York since the middle of the 13th century. Thomas Wolsey, as Archbishop, had started to build as soon as he was elevated to the see of York and by 1519-20 had begun to expand beyond the original site and to buy neighbouring land. A stray reference in a letter of 1528 alludes to the erection of the great hall 'with other edifices there, being now in building'.[4] As the house was part of the temporal possessions of the see of York, the means by which it came into the grasping hands of Henry VIII were devious. On October 29th, 1529, Wolsey was deprived of the Great Seal and, acknowledging praemunire, he asked the King to take his temporal possessions:

'Then went my lord and Called all officers in euery office in his howsse byfore hyme, to take accompte of all suche stuffe as they had in charge. And in his Gallery there was sett dyuers tables where vppon (were laid) a great nomber of Richestuffe . . . ffurthermore ther was also the walles of the gallery hanged with clothes of gold and tissue of dyuers makyinges and clothe of syluer lykewyse on bothe the sydes and riche clothes of Baudkyn of dyuers Colours . . . Than had he in ij Chambers adioynyng to the Gallery, thoon called the gylt Chamber and thother called most Comenly the Councell chamber . . . In the gylt Chamber was sett owt vppon the tables nothing but all gylt plate; And vppon a Cupbord standyng vnder a wyndowe was garnysshed all holy with plate of cleane gold wherof Somme was sett with peerle and riche stones. And in the Councell chamber was set all wyght plate and parcell gylt. And vnder the tables in bothe the Chambers were sett baskettes with old plate whiche was not estemed but for broken plate and old not worthy to be occupied'.[5]

Cavendish's memorable account of his master's removal conjures up the glory of York Place under Wolsey. Three months after, the King was in possession announcing his intention of elevating it to the rank of a royal palace.

The conversion of York Place into the Palace of Westminster, soon to be known as White-Hall, was carried through, like the King's later Nonsuch project, with enormous speed. It was complete enough by the autumn of 1533 to receive Anne Boleyn as Queen.

The exterior was never impressive. A visiting Italian in 1531 alludes to it as being 'without much architecture as is usual in all the buildings of this country'.[6] Caustic comment indeed, but inevitable from the pen of a man familiar with the achievements of Alberti and

1 There is no satisfactory account of Tudor Whitehall. Fundamental is the LCC *Survey of London,* ed, M. H. Cox and P. Norman, X–XIII, The Parish of St Margaret, Westminster, parts I, II, III, London, 1926, 1930, 1931. These do not make full use of any of the surviving building accounts. They are: P.R.O.E. 36/251; E. 36/252; E. 351 3322; B. M. Royal MS 14 B. IV A and B. E. Sheppard, *The Old Royal Palace of Whitehall,* London, 1902 is virtually useless. Per Palme, *Triumph of Peace,* London, 1957, although definitive on the Inigo Jones banqueting house, is none the less valuable for the Tudor period. A recent general book is G. S. Dugdale, *Whitehall through the Ages,* London, 1950.

2 *A Harmony of Essays, etc. of Francis Bacon,* ed. E. Arber, English Reprints, London 1871, pp548 ff.

3 The view expressed by Count Magalotti when he visited the palace in the train of Cosimo III, Grand Duke of Tuscany. For quotations of this and other similar 17th century views, see Palme, *Triumph of Peace,* p102 note 2.

4 Fox to Gardiner, 11th May 1528, *Letters and Papers,* 1526-28. p1872

5 George Cavendish, *The Life and Death of Cardinal Wolsey,* ed. R. S. Sylvester, Early English Text Society, London, 1959, pp98-99.

6 *Calendar of State Papers,* Venetian, IV, p171.

Brunelleschi. Humanism in letters had penetrated England but its attendant theories on architectural proportion had to await Inigo Jones and the Whitehall banqueting house. Nonsuch alone of Henry's projects arose from its foundations as a palace, and it would be wrong to expect his hasty adaptation of a bishop's town house to reflect a similar architectural unity. Wolsey had begun by remodelling and extending the group of buildings by the riverside. Henry followed suit by purchasing large tracts of land, chiefly to the west, thereby enabling the creation of a park and pleasure gardens. But even he was unable, in spite of the purchase and demolition of hundreds of houses, to destroy or deny the ancient public right of way to the riverside or through the palace itself from north to south. Making a virtue of necessity, these very irksome features were transformed into the pivots of his grandest additions, the three great gateways: that in and out of King Street, that giving admittance to the court itself, and the pathway which led to the river Thames. They were to bear testimony to those that used them that here the new Constantine had made his residence.

Payments to tentmakers who erected a canvas house over 'the newe gate' to enable the workmen to continue labouring in all weathers, dues to riders who traversed the realm for masons for the King's service, and candles to enable painters to work at night, give an indication of the haste that attended the work.[1] The Court Gate seems to have been of the normal early Tudor red-brick type, familiar through surviving examples at Hampton Court, but the King Street gates were more unusual. The so-called Holbein Gate [Plate 18] was of chequered flint and brick work with the royal arms over the archway and Tudor rose and portcullis badges. Four terracotta roundels of Roman Emperors set into the wall surface

1 P.R.O.E. 351/3322 records a canvas house over 'the newe gate' for work to continue and canvas 'to hange before the worke made by paynters vppon the Galerie walles'.

Plate 18   George Vertue
The so-called Holbein Gate
Engraving

Plate 19   George Vertue
The King Street Gate
Engraving

gave the entrance a suitable 'imperial' overtone. Finally came the last and most imaginative of the gateways [Plate 19], a curious rectangular building, two storeys in height; with Doric and Ionic orders, flanked by two domed towers and adorned with antique busts grouped around a central one encircled by half the band of the zodiac.

The inspiration for this gateway was French.[1] Historians have long been aware that the dominating influence on Henry's later palaces was Fontainebleau, Chambord and the other French royal châteaux, but there is evidence that Henry was already apeing Francis I at Whitehall. The octagonal tower of the cockpit with its lantern, pinnacles and onion dome directly anticipates the towers of Nonsuch, and these in turn may stem back to Chambord which was begun in 1519[2]. And Whitehall, too, was, at least in part, decorated with antique plaster-work on its exterior walls. This again is a rehearsal for the full-blown fantasies of Nonsuch: 'As for *Grotesco* or (as we say) *Antique-worke*', writes Sanderson in 1658, 'It takes my fancy, though in forms of different Natures, or *Sexes, Sirenes, Centaures*, and such like, as the outward walls of *White-Hall*, observes this kind; as running-trale-work; and not ill-mastered . . .'[3] If we wish to gain an impression of the appearance of this 'antique work' we should peer through the left-hand doorway of the Group picture of Henry VIII enthroned with his family [Plate 20]. In the distance, behind the gesturing maid servant, part of White-hall Palace can be seen adorned from the ground level up with panels of antique grotesque-work.[4]

The remaining preponderant architectural theme was also French. No less than three great galleries formed the axes upon which the palace depended. One linked the privy lodgings by way of the Holbein Gateway with the tiltyard. This, known as the Privy Gallery, was a re-erection of Cardinal Wolsey's gallery at Esher (again evidence of the rush); the taking away of the gallery, writes Cavendish, 'byfore my lordes face was to hyme a corrysife'.[5] The two others ran due south from the privy lodgings, the lower known as the Orchard Gallery and the upper as the Stone Gallery. The Low or Orchard Gallery was an adaptation of an existing gallery, the windows being altered and the gallery adorned by wall paintings. These and the Privy Gallery overlooked an orchard which remained until the very last years of the reign. Later this orchard became the privy garden occupying an area later to become famous as the site of the Sermon Court. The garden was situated throughout the fifteen thirties on the other side of the palace.

From the outside these, then, were the most striking features, but what of the palace interior? Von Wedel, a German visitor of 1584, is one of many who held the view that there were 'several of a finer exterior, but the latter did not equal this on the inside'. The interior was 'very beautiful and royal indeed'.[6] The earliest and most complete account of it in the early Tudor period is by a visiting condottiere of literary bent, one Mario Savorgnano, Count of Belgrade, in 1531.

'I saw a palace, built by the late Cardinal, which now belongs to the King, together with other property of that prelate. The building is now being enlarged; and I saw three so-called 'galleries', which are long porticos and halls, without chambers, with windows on each side, looking on gardens and rivers, the ceiling being marvellously wrought in stone with gold, and the wainscot of carved wood representing a thousand beautiful figures; and round about there are chambers, and very large halls, all hung with tapestries'.[7]

If we wish to supplement this general impression of the staggering opulence of the state

Plate 20   Artist unknown
View of the Privy Garden at Whitehall Palace
Detail from *The Family of Henry VIII*
Reproduced by gracious permission of Her Majesty the Queen

1 See J. Summerson, *Architecture in Britain*, p8.

2 A. Blunt, *Art and Architecture in France, 1500-1700*, London, 1953, p27 ff.

3 N. Sanderson, *Graphice*, London, 1658, p25.

4 O. Millar, *The Tudor, Stuart and Early Georgian Pictures in the Collection of Her Majesty the Queen*, London, 1963, I, pp63-64 (43).

5 A. Cavendish, *Life of Wolsey*, ed. cit, p 123

6 *Journey through England and Scotland made by Lupold von Wedel in the years 1584 and 1585*, Transactions of the Royal Historical Society, new series, IX, 1895, p237. The Duke of Stettin-Pomerania in 1602 is less enthusiastic even on the interior: 'the lodgments in this palatio are almost all low, and constructed with many recesses after the monkish way of building', *Diary of the Journey of Philip Julius, Duke of Stettin-Pomerania*, ed. G. von Bülow, Transactions of the Royal Historical Society, new series, VI, 1892, p23.

7 *Calendar of State Papers*, Venetian, IV, 1527-33, pp286-87.

Plate 21   Probably after John Raff (?Joannes Corvus) and his assistants *The Embarkation for Boulogne*
$66\frac{1}{2} \times 135\frac{3}{4}$ inches
Reproduced by gracious permission of Her Majesty the Queen

1 The inventories are (i) P.R.O.E. 351/160 (Miscellaneous Books of the Augmentation Office.) This was compiled in 1542 on the appointment of Sir Anthony Denny as Keeper of the Palace of Westminster and is concerned solely with the contents of that palace. (ii) Harleian MS. 1419 A and B. (Inventories taken in 1547 on the death of Henry VIII of the contents of all the royal palaces.) Occasionally there is listing by room.

rooms, there are inventories of the contents of the palace taken in 1542 and in 1547.[1] These confirm that the impact was heightened by an abundant use of rich hangings of 'cloth of tissue, cloth of golde, baudkyn and vellat', all encrusted with gold embroidery representing the king's arms and badges. Great sets of Flemish tapestries are listed: the Months, the Story of David and Absolom, the Acts of the Apostles, the Sabines, the Seven Virtues, the Story of Cupid. Verdure hangings transformed rooms into bowers of greenery and in the solemn apartments of state hung cloths of estate, all bearing 'the kinges armes crowned holden by his maiesties bestis with a garlond'. The list continues, a phantasmagoria of ostentation; chairs, cushions and carpets, on through bedsteads, linen, pictures, mirrors and musical instruments, to plate and chapel furnishings. Reading such an inventory is an admirable corrective to visualising Whitehall in the light of the few remaining bleak rooms at Hampton Court. It is undeniable that in spite of all the splendour of the ceilings and carved woodwork, the ultimate *coup de theatre* was achieved through moveables and that everything was but a variation on a single theme, gold. The ceilings were gold, the panelling was picked out in gold, gold thread ran through the tapestries, the fabric hangings and upholstery were gold or shot with gold, the utensils were almost all gold or silver gilt and everywhere and on everything there was massive heavy gold embroidery and fringing. Reflected in the shafts of sunlight, streaming through the mullioned windows, or glistening by the light of a hundred candles at night, it must have seemed almost celestial. No one who saw it could doubt that it had achieved Henry's ambition, as defined in the Act of Parliament concerning the palace, to create 'many and syngvler commodious thyngs, pleasurs and other

Plate 22   Probably after John Raff (?Joannes Corvus) and his assistants *The Field of Cloth of Gold*
$66\frac{1}{2} \times 135\frac{7}{8}$ inches
Reproduced by gracious permission of Her Majesty the Queen

necessaryes, most apt and convenyent to apperteyne only to so noble a prynce, for his syngvler comforte, passetyme and solace'.[1]

One of the great galleries to which Savorgnano alludes was adorned with a series of wall paintings. This, which the accounts refer to as the 'gallarye altrid', ran at ground level beneath the new Stone Gallery and overlooked the orchard. The alterations took the form of remodelling the windows and introducing frescoes depicting 'The Coronation of our saide Sovereigne', later referred to as 'King Henryes Coronation and his going to Bulleyne (Boulogne)'.[2] Although over fifty artists laboured on these paintings – an important indication of their size – the painter presiding was apparently John Raff, perhaps identical with Joannes Corvus, painter of the portrait of Bishop Fox at Corpus Christi College, Oxford.[3] If we are to understand Holbein's contribution to the decoration of Whitehall it is very necessary to elicit what exactly these paintings executed under Joannes Corvus's supervision, and probably after his design, looked like. They will provide the vital yardstick whereby we shall be able to judge the originality or otherwise of Holbein's great work.

The problem of these paintings is perhaps not as insoluble as it would seem on the surface. The crucial clue is the reference to 'his going to Boulogne', for this could only refer to the famous crossing of 1520, the occasion of the meeting outside Guisnes of Henry VIII and Francis I, known as the Field of Cloth of Gold. Its choice for Whitehall, along with the Coronation, was obvious, for no other event had better manifested to the world the King's desire to be seen as the perfect, chivalrous, warrior prince. Two surviving pictures depict these very events, *The Embarkation for Boulogne* and the *Field of Cloth of Gold* itself [Plate

1 LCC Survey, St Margaret, Westminster, II, i, p21.

2 E. Croft-Murray, *Decorative Painting in England, 1537-1837*, London, 1962, I, p163 lists the artists involved. The evidence is admittedly confusing. In the Henrician accounts the Coronation is the only subject actually specified although it is clear that there were others: 'In drawing and settyng with colours the coronation of our seide souereigne lorde with the circumstancee of the same. As also *certayne other workes* (italics mine) vppon the walles of the newe galerie . . .' (P.R.O.E. 351/3322). These are not referred to again and presumably quickly perished. The next reference comes to the varnishing of 'all the discourse of King Henries Coronacion and his going to Bulleyne' (P.R.O.E. 351/3223) in the Presence Chamber in 1588-89. They were clearly considered as a series and the Coronation provides the link back to the Orchard Gallery frescoes, the others very plausibly qualifying as copies of the 'certayne other workes'.
An account of the use of this gallery for a fete in 1559 implies that it was an open arcade or or loggia. *Calendar of State Papers*, Venetian, 1558-80, pp91-92.

3 E. Auerbach, *Tudor Artists*, London, 1954, p160; pp13-14 on the gallery.

1 Catalogued in O. Millar, *Catalogue* I, pp54-56 (nos. 24-25).

2 Ibid, p55. See note 1. on previous page.

21, 22].[1] Until now they have always been regarded as paintings executed late in Henry VIII's reign but there is no trace of them in the exhaustive inventory of the various royal palaces made on his death in 1547. They first appear in 1588-9, along with one of the Coronation, in the Presence Chamber when 'all the discourse of King Henries Coronacon and his going to Bulleyne' was varnished with a special varnish.[2] In other words, by the end of the Elizabethan period there was a set of pictures in the Presence Chamber linked in subject to those which once made up the wall paintings in the Orchard Gallery. The conclusion to be drawn that the pictures now at Hampton Court are Elizabethan copies of two of the lost Orchard Gallery frescoes is irresistible and surely correct. In the first place, they are on canvas which suggests a later date, in the second, on grounds of style, they hardly connect with surviving instances of Tudor narrative pictures, such as the Battle of Spurs, which are recorded in early inventories. There is, too, the undeniable fact that Henry VIII is dressed in costume neither of 1520, nor of 1540, but of 1530 and, a final fact to clinch the argument, all references to Catherine of Aragon, the divorced Queen, have been suppressed. These paintings celebrate the events of 1520 as seen through the political eyes of 1530. Adorning a broad frieze above the panelling of the Orchard Gallery, the original frescoes by Corvus and his assistants must indeed have been superb decoration.

Yet we must also look at them critically as examples of renaissance wall decoration and as such no one can deny that they belong to the past, to the dying embers of medievalism. Separate events are synthesised into one overall pattern of activity, resulting in such nonsensical happenings as Henry VIII's procession riding out of the town of Guisnes and back into its castle. There is also no apparent attempt to integrate it with its architectural surround. They remain fundamentally materialisations in paint of the brilliant, transitory world of festival evoked by Hall in his *Chronicle*. If one had to choose a parallel to the Orchard Gallery frescoes it would be Benozzo Gozzoli's journey of the Magi in the Medici Chapel in the Palazzo Medici Riccardi. Just five years later Holbein was to introduce the court to the principles of high renaissance illusionistic wall painting. It remains an astounding fact that the early Tudor court, during the decade 1530 to 1540, was able to telescope in the space of so many years the artistic development of so many decades. This acceleration can be paralleled elsewhere, for instance, in carved relief decoration by a comparison between the choir screen on King's College Chapel, Cambridge [Plate 23] constructed under royal auspices between 1531 and 1535, and the carved work that appears in a lost design for a Presence Chamber, circa 1543–47 [Plate 24]. The former consists of pilasters and friezes in the chaste early renaissance style, the latter of florid caryatids, fruits swags and giant cartouches. Within ten years Henry VIII's court had moved out of a late lingering medievalism, on through a transitory moment of renaissance classicism to find itself finally in the embrace of mannerism at its most bizarre.

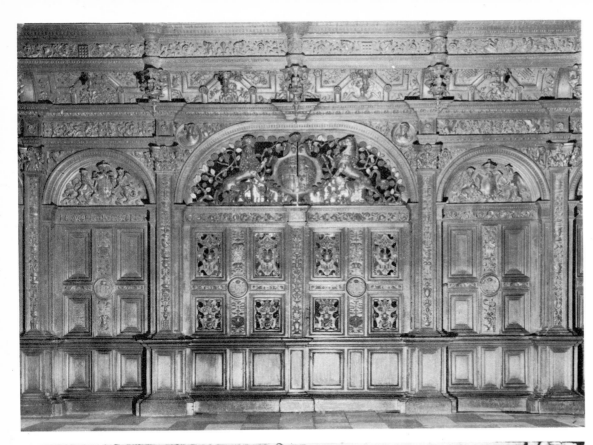

Plate 23   *Choir Screen, King's College Chapel, Cambridge*

Plate 24   Attributed to Nicolò da Modena
Design for a Presence Chamber
Present whereabouts unknown

THE PRIVY CHAMBER

*' THIS CHAMBER is always styled
HONOURABLE, but properly should be called,
as it is at present, MOST HONOURABLE.'*

Nicholas Carlisle, 1829[1]

[1]Nicholas Carlisle, *An Inquiry into the Place and Quality of the Gentlemen of His Majesty's most Honourable Privy Chamber*, London, 1829, p35b.

All Tudor and Stuart palaces were governed by the same fundamental room sequence, one which was repeated even in improvised form while the court was on progress. Both King and Consort had to have their own separate Guard Chamber, Presence Chamber and Privy Chamber.[1] In the case of Whitehall Palace there were a distinct King's and Queen's side, a feature which is clear under the Stuarts but confused under the Tudors due to the rule of two Queens regnant, who would have used the King's side, and an unmarried boy King. The location of the consort's rooms is open to doubt but they seem to have opened off the privy gallery and were part of the Council Chamber block but the King's or Sovereign's state apartments definitely occupied the block running parallel to the river. A great flight of stone steps at the north-east corner led up to the Guard or Great Chamber, where the Yeomen of the Guard, the King's personal bodyguard, were in constant attendance; beyond lay the Presence Chamber, a large room with a gilt ceiling, dominated by a throne and canopy. All who could lay claim to the rank of gentleman had access here and the Presence was always thronged with courtiers and those seeking patronage and favour awaiting the entry of the Sovereign from the Privy Chamber beyond.

The Presence Chamber was the grand *salon de reception* of the Tudor period, thrown into greater relief by the absence until 1581 of a state banqueting house. In that year Elizabeth built one on what was to be the site for Inigo Jones's later structure and from then on it became the most important room for state receptions. But prior to 1581 we are back in the heyday of the Presence Chamber and it is around this room and its use that the delicately graded nuances of court ceremonial centre. The greatest honour a visitor could be accorded was to be met by the reigning sovereign in the Guard Chamber and to proceed from there to the Presence. Mary in this way honoured her cousin Cardinal Pole, come to reconcile England to the Holy See,[2] and five years later, in 1559, her sister Elizabeth similarly greeted the French Commissioners come to ratify the Treaty of Câteau-Cambrésis.[3] This was exceptional. An ambassador normally was conducted to the Presence Chamber to present his credentials, the Sovereign seated enthroned with government officials standing either side and the whole court ablaze in gala costume forming a lane up to the dais. After the King had read the document he would hand it over to his secretary of state and bid the ambassador cover. Formal compliments were then exchanged after which the Ambassador presented his suite who made their obeisances and kissed hands. This accomplished the Ambassador and his train departed.[4]

The Privy Chamber was in itself a moderately recent innovation, evolved in the late fifteenth century, when the establishment of a separate Inner and Outer Chamber each with its own staffs emerged.[5] Just as, at an earlier period, the king had retreated from the Hall to the Presence Chamber, so now, with the increasing elaboration and luxury of court life, it split in two, into an outer public Presence Chamber and an inner private Privy Chamber. Grooms for both were in existence early on in the reign but the Gentlemen of the Privy Chamber were a later innovation, based, perhaps, on a French court model. These were established as a definite class by the Eltham Articles of 1526.[6] The Articles, an effort by Cardinal Wolsey to check chaos and establish order in the Royal Household, are the foundations of Tudor and Stuart court etiquette. In relation to the Privy Chamber there had been a scandal some seven years before in 1519 when 'certain young men in his privie chamber, not regardyng his estate nor degree, were so familiar and homely with hym, and plaied suche light touches with hym that they forgat themselfes'. The Council caused the

[1] This is discussed in L. Hotson, *The First Night of Twelfth Night*, London, 1954, pp173 ff.

[2] *Calendar of State Papers*, Spanish, 1554-58, pp118-19.
[3] *Calendar of State Papers*, Venetian, 1558-80, p91.

[4] See S. Palme, *Triumph of Peace* pp154-65.

[5] See E. K. Chambers, *The Elizabethan Stage*, Oxford, 1951, ed, I, pp42-44 and especially p43, note 1.

[6] The Statutes of Eltham are reprinted in *Antiquarian Repertory*, London, 1808, III, pp141-46.

1 *Henry VIII by Edward Hall* ed C. Whibley, London, 1904, pp177-78.

Lord Chamberlain to banish these gentlemen from the court and appointed in their stead 'foure sad and auncient knightes'.[1] Wolsey's Articles sought to regulate the routine of the Household and central to all his provisions was the sanctity of the Privy Chamber. The Articles state categorically:

'. . . that the Kinges Heighnesse have his Priveye Chamber and inwarde lodgeinges reserved secrete, to the pleasure of his Grace, without repayre of any greate multitude unto it. It is therefore ordayned, that no persone of what state, degree or conditione soever he be, from henceforthe presume, attempte, or be in any wise suffered or admitted to come or repayre in to the Kinge's Priuye Chamber . . .'[2]

2 *Antiquarian Repertory*, III, p141.

Six Gentlemen, two Gentlemen Ushers, four Grooms, a barber and a page were bound to render 'humble, reverend, secrett and comelye service'. They waited and attended upon the King at all times. Between six and seven every morning the Grooms repaired to the Chamber to sweep and clean it and to light the fire. Here on arising His Majesty was ceremonially dressed; here he usually ate, and here too he transacted most of the business of the day. At night two of the Gentlemen slept on pallet beds on the Privy Chamber floor both to minister to and protect the King.

No detailed description or drawing of the interior of the Privy Chamber at Whitehall Palace is known to exist. The most detailed account is by a visiting Frenchman, Monsieur de Maisse, come to woo Elizabeth I into alignment with Henry IV in 1597.[3] De Maisse arrived in London in December when the court was in residence at Whitehall, which Elizabeth reached customarily each year in time for the annual tournament held on her Accession Day, November 17th, and where she held her Christmas Revels. The fact that he was received in the Privy Chamber at all was due to the Queen 'Having caught a cold in her teeth'. It was more likely intended to be a deliberate snub, for all ambassadors were received in state in the Presence. On December 8th De Maisse was summoned by a gentleman of the court to an audience. Led to the riverside, he found a barge sent by the Queen to convey him by water to Whitehall where he landed at the palace stairs and was met by the future Sir Henry Wotton attended by five other gentlemen. He describes how he was led through the Great Chamber, a room 'of moderate size', into the Presence Chamber where he waited. In due course the Lord Chamberlain, Henry Carey, 2nd Lord Hunsdon, appeared and conducted him to the Queen:

3 *A Journal of all that was accomplished by Monsieur de Maisse* . . . , ed. G. B. Harrison and R. A. Jones, London, 1931, pp22 ff. on his reception. He states (p27) that Whitehall 'is very low and has no great appearance for a royal house'.

'He led me along a passage somewhat dark, into a Chamber that they call the Privy Chamber, at the head of which was the Queen seated in a low chair, by herself, and withdrawn from all the Lords and Ladies that were present, they being in one place and she in another. After I had made my reverence at the entry of the chamber, she rose and came five or six paces towards me, almost into the middle of the chamber'.[4]

4 Ibid, p23

De Maisse bent down and kissed the hem of her robe after which she embraced him with both hands. Soon she had returned to her chair and De Maisse was given a stool nearby on which he sat talking to her. On the conclusion of the audience De Maisse presented the gentlemen of his train who reverenced her in turn, Elizabeth embracing them all 'with great charm and smiling countenance'. De Maisse then goes on to tell us a little more about the room:

'In this chamber called the Privy Chamber, which resembles somewhat a closet, and in which there is no bed (he is thinking of the French court where credentials were presented in the bedchamber), there were several ladies (presumably the Ladies of the Privy Chamber), as also in the Presence Chamber, but not many; the chief men of her Council also were there, that is to say, the Lord Treasurer (William Cecil, Lord Burghley) who is carried in a chair and is very old and white; the Admiral (Charles Howard, Lord Howard of Effingham and Earl of Nottingham); (Sir Robert) Cecil, Secretary of State; (Thomas Sackville) Lord Buckhurst, Councillor of State, all of whom I saluted as I went out and promised to visit'.[1]

As upon his entry he was led from the Privy Chamber to the Presence by the Lord Chamberlain, where, in turn, Wotton awaited to conduct De Maisse to his barge. On several subsequent occasions De Maisse was conducted to the Queen in the Privy Chamber in such a way; on one occasion he found her standing by a window, on another having the spinet played to her.

De Maisse's narrative is supplemented a little by the description from the journal of the Duke of Saxe-Weimar who visited England in 1613. He describes the room as being entirely hung with tapestries and goes on to give the earliest certain reference we have by any visitor to the Holbein wall-painting: 'Whole-length Portraits of Henry VIII, and his father Henry VII. These are considered remarkably artistic, and they say that there is nothing like them in England'.[2] Concerning the furnishings, we can gather two fragments from the inventories taken of the palace five years before and on the occasion of Henry VIII's death. Unfortunately in the case of Whitehall, the listing is under subject and not room by room but two articles are specifically stated to be in the King's Privy Chamber. The first is a hanging:

'Item a Ceeler oonly of a cloth of Estate serving for a hanging within the king his graces privey Chamber of cloth of gold tissue reysed with purple vellat purled paned with crymsen vellat enbraudered vpon the said crymsen vellat his graces badges Crowned And in the middes therof his hignes Armes crowned holden by his bestes within a Garland enbraudered vpon hit being in length iij yerdes and in bredth two yerdes quarter lyned with buckeram With Six single vallaunces of like stuff and Workmanship likewise lyned . . .'[3]

The second is an elaborate and costly little fountain:

'In the kinges prevye chamber
Item ther is sett into the walle in the previe chambre a thinge artificiallie made like a worke wherein is many straunge deuisses of fruers and diuerse other things having in it a fountayne of allablaster whiche is sore decayed and vppon the toppe of the fountayne a rounde Balle of christall wherein was three heddes of golde whiche are gone and xiij stones made like heddes also gone whiche was supposed to be Camewes being sett aboute in a Border everyone of the compasse of a grote all whiche fountayne and work is locked vpp with two Leaves like windowes the whiche leaves are garneshed with peerle and golde threde purled'.[4]

Both items give an adequate impression of the sumptuousness of the decor but the prime impression is one of a small room hung all round with tapestries. Furniture would have been limited, as indeed it was in most Tudor palaces, and the focal point must have been a chair of estate. Some indication of the furnishings may be gathered by lists of some of the items in the Privy Chambers at two other palaces, Greenwich and Hampton Court. At Greenwich

[1] Ibid, pp26-27.

[2] J. W. Neumayr von Ramssla, *Des Durchlaughtigen hochgeborgnen*, Leipzig, 1620, p177; Rye, *England as seen by Foreigners*, pp160-61 gives a partial transcript.

[3] P.R.O.E. 351/160 f. 12; by 1547 this had been removed to the Garderobe of the Tower, B.M. Harleian MS.1419A.f.29

[4] B. M. Harleian MS 1419 B.f.516ᵛ. The Privy Chamber at Nonsuch had a costly fountain in the form of a silver serpent under the foot of a lion, J. Dent, *Nonsuch*, p103.

1 B. M. Harleian MS 1419. A.f.54, p244ᵛ.

2 V. von Klarwill, *Queen Elizabeth and Some Foreigners*, London, 1928 contains descriptions of receptions in the Privy Chamber in 1595 for an envoy of the Duke of Würtemberg, pp363 ff.

3 P. Fraser Tytler, *England under the Reigns of Edward VI and Mary*, London, 1839, I, pp284-90.

4 R. Strong, *Queen Elizabeth I and the Order of the Garter*, Archaeological Journal, CXIX, 1964, p250.

5 Sir John Finett, *Finetti Philoxensis*, London, 1656 contains many references to ambassadors dining with James I in the Privy Chamber.

there was 'a Brekefaste table of wallnot tree', 'a rounde table covered with blacke vellat', 'a square table', 'a Cuppbourde of waynescotte', a pair of regals, stalls and forms to sit upon. At Hampton Court there was 'one payre of portatives with the Kinge and the Quene Ianes Armes', 'two cubbordes of wainscotte', 'one table covered with grene clothe', 'two joyned formes', 'iij joyned Stooles', a bracket to sit a clock on, a 'deske of black lether,' a candlestick, fire-irons, and a leather case.[1] These lists strike an extremely domestic note and epitomise admirably the nodal point that the Privy Chamber occupied in palace etiquette forming a bridge between the public and private aspects of the King's life. It was a room which could be shifted in mood either way, towards the totally informal, or, on semi-state occasions, with a swift mustering of its officers it could easily become the scene of 'informal' formal receptions.[2]

In short, those narratives tell us that here, as the Eltham Articles imply, the monarch passed his time during the day and transacted most of the affairs of state. As far as the court was concerned, access to the Privy Chamber in the Tudor period remained the prerogative of the few. Occasionally highly honoured persons would dine there: Edward VI entertained the French commissioners in 1550,[3] Queen Elizabeth regaled her Knights of the Garter with supper on their feast day[4] and James I dined ambassadors at his table.[5] But it remained first and foremost the most important of the Monarch's private suite of rooms. In the Presence Chamber and beyond he lived out, amidst the etiquette of the court, his public life; in the Privy Chamber, untrammelled for the most part by the rigid ceremonial that conditioned his life in the state rooms, he passed most of his private life.

SOME MONUMENT OF VERTUE

'*Semblable deckynge oughte to be in the house of a
noble man or man of honour. I meane concernynge
ornamentes of halle and chambres, in Arise, painted
tables, and images containyng histories, wherin
is represented some monument of vertue, moste
cunnyngly wroughte . . .*'

Sir Thomas Eylot, *The Governour*[1]

[1]Sir Thomas Elyot, *The Boke named the
Gouernour*, ed. H. H. S. Croft, London, 1880,
II, pp22–24.

Plate 25   Remigius van Leemput after Holbein
Copy of The Privy Chamber Wall-painting
35 × 38⅞ inches Reproduced by gracious permission
of Her Majesty the Queen

Plate 26   Remigius van Leemput after Holbein
Copy of the Privy Chamber Wall-painting
35 × 40 inches The Lord Egremont Petworth House

34

The two copies through which the final form of the wall painting is known are by Remigius or Remée van Leemput, an artist of Flemish or French extraction who worked, for the most part, as a copyist in the Restoration period. The copy still in the Royal Collection was deliberately commissioned by Charles II in 1667 as a record [Plate 25][1] and two years later Leemput painted a second copy, probably for the Seymour family, which is now at Petworth House [Plate 26].[2] The latter has slight variations, namely the introduction of the Seymour coat of arms, in place of the verses on the marble altar, together with the figure of the young Edward VI, a likeness taken from a portrait at Petworth House.[3] Vertue later records that Leemput made two further copies of the figures of Henry VIII and Henry VII.[4] Finally, in 1737, Vertue himself was to execute an elaborate watercolour after the Royal Collection version for his engraving of the wall painting [Plate 2].[5] Neither of the Leemput copies can be rated as being of more than antiquarian interest. That they were highly regarded at the time, however, is reflected in Buckeridge's record that Leemput was paid the sum of £150 for the copy he made for Charles II.[6]

The scene both copies set is as follows. On either side of a stone altar are grouped Henry VII and his wife, Elizabeth of York, and Henry VIII and his third Queen, Jane Seymour. They are standing on a stepped platform which has been built around an altar or block of stone, the upper level bearing the parents, the lower the son and his wife. The upper platform continues behind the altar as the turkey carpet which has been placed on it, finding its passage interrupted, falls around the altar in rich folds. All four persons are elaborately and splendidly attired. Henry VII and Elizabeth of York are wearing golden costumes, lavishly trimmed and lined with ermine; he rests an arm on a cushion placed on top of the altar while she sustains, with one hand, the heavy weight of her skirts. Jane Seymour, a shy figure, her hands clasped before her, wears a dress of tawny gold, a petticoat and false undersleeves of crimson velvet, the turn-back of her oversleeves of ermine and her bodice swagged with ropes of pearl. On her bodice is an IHS monogram jewel that must be identical with one recorded in a contemporary inventory:

'a ffaire IHUS of dyamondes set in golde conteyning xxiij small dyamondes iij litle emoraldes and a small Rubie having also iij perles ij lesse and i more hanging thereat'.[7]

A little dog nestles on her train. Directly opposite her, Henry stands, facing the spectator, his legs stretched widely apart, in his right hand gloves, his left holding the cord of his

1 O. Millar, Catalogue, I, p117. It is inscribed, signed and dated:
PROTOTYPVM IVSTAE MAGNITVDINIS IPSO OPERE TECTORIO/FECIT HOLBENIVS IVBENTE HENRICO VIII./ ECTYPVM A REMIGIO VAN LEEMPUT BREVIORI TABELLA/DESCRIBI VOLVIT CAROLVS II.M.B.F.E.H.R. A° DNI. MDCLXVII.

2 C. H. Collins Baker *Catalogue of the Petworth Collection* 1920, p72 (347).

3 Ibid, p58 (370).

4 G. Vertue, *Notebooks*, I, Walpole Society, XVIII, 1930, p56. Oliver Millar suggests, op. cit, loc. cit, that the Henry VII and Henry VIII at Drayton (Stopford-Sackville coll.) may be identical with one.

5 A. P. Oppé, *English Drawings* at *Windsor Castle* London, 1950, p98 (625).

6 H. Buckeridge, *An Essay towards an English School* in the English edition of de Piles *Art of Painting*, London, 1706, pp435, 548.

7 B. M. Royal MS. Appendix 89.f.33.

Plate 27   Unknown artist *Henry VII*
Private collection

Plate 28   Unknown artist *Elizabeth of York*
21½ × 15¾ inches
National Portrait Gallery, London

dagger. Both his golden brown doublet and his fur-lined surcoat are slashed and embroidered with gold thread. Splendid jewels are worn: a great pendant at the end of a chain of gold, jewels set in gold mounts securing the slashings on his doublet and sleeves, and, above all, a great carcanet of balas rubies and pearls. The latter was still preserved as late as 1606 as yet unbroken amongst the Crown Jewels:

'Item, one Coller of gould, set with nine very great ballaces in collets of gould, and ten knots of pearls, every knot containing sixteen pearls'.[1]

Behind this solemn group rises an ornate architectural background of rich, multi-coloured marbles. Two shell-niches flank a central arch and are divided from each other by elaborately carved pilasters. Between the capitals of the pilasters runs a freize in high relief of mermen

1 J. Nichols, *Progresses of James I*, London, 1828, II, p46.

36

and mermaids supporting cartouches inscribed with the year and date of the composition: ANNO 1537. Above them, in turn, two brackets protrude on which sit the royal supporters, the lion and the dragon, each holding shields bearing the royal arms and beyond them, in the distance, further arches arise. It is not difficult to imagine that the effect of this blown large, with a lavish use of gold leaf, must indeed have been one of glittering richness.

The miraculous survival of the Chatsworth Cartoon [Plate 1], now in the National Portrait Gallery,[1] containing the left hand half of the composition, captures that sublime magic of line and intricacy of detail which must also have made up two of the unforgettable features of the Group in its final form. The technique of the Cartoon follows that which is typical of Holbein's work, the preparation of a detailed, actual-sized, drawing of the whole composition which was pin-pricked and transferred to the surface to be painted. The Cartoon is made up in exactly the same way as the large cartoon for his later project, Henry VIII and the Barber-Surgeons Company.[2] The figures of Henry VII and Henry VIII are drawn in black ink with a brush on to large sheets of paper, cut out and mounted, collage-fashion, on to a huge sheet of paper bearing the architectural background. In the Cartoon the figures are tinted with thin watercolour washes of purplish-brown, brown and black.[3] The whole procedure is typical of a method for which we have the earliest evidence in Italy in the second half of the 14th century. It is not until over a century later that the pricked cartoon figure becomes the norm, carrying into practice Alberti's dictum that objects must be drawn 'as if equal in representation to that which you wish to compose . . . in small drawings it is easy to hide great faults; in the large the smallest faults are easily seen'.[4]

All the portraits are initially based on ones already in existence; those of Henry VII and Elizabeth of York on patterns which continued to be copied and multiplied for the remainder of the century, those of Henry and Jane on portraits painted by Holbein the year before the wall painting was finished. The parents present no problems [Plates 27, 28], although it is interesting to note that neither the work of Torrigiani, nor the funeral effigies in Westminster Abbey were drawn upon.[5] Holbein probably worked his figures up from the two portraits recorded in the 1542 Royal Inventory:

'Item a table with the picture of Kynge Henry the seventh with a curten of yellow and white sarconet paned together:

'Item a table with the picture of Quene Elizabeth with a curten of yellow and white sarconet paned together'.[6]

In the case of Henry and Jane the key portraits are those now in the Thyssen Collection [Plate 29] and the Mauritshuis [Plate 32] respectively, both almost identical in size and almost certainly to be equated with an item likewise listed in the Inventory of 1542: 'Item, a table like a booke, with the picture of Kyng Henry the eight and Quene Jane'.[7]

Another version of the portrait of Jane Seymour, showing more of the figure, exists in Vienna [Plate 32] and the original drawing for both is in the Royal Collection at Windsor.[8] Allowing for an alteration of dress, there seems little doubt that this is the basis for the full length in the Group. 'She is . . .', wrote Chapuys to Antoine Perrenot, 'of middle stature, and no great beauty, so fair that one would call her rather pale than otherwise'.[9] The King's own portrait as it appears initially in the Cartoon was likewise a derivative of the sitting given for the diptych [Plate 33], although in the final version the face is turned outwards. This implies a new sitting by the King, probably the last one Henry ever granted, as the

1 On the descent of the cartoon see the Appendix, p81.

2 R. Strong, Holbein's Cartoon for the Barber-Surgeons Group Rediscovered – A Preliminary Report, Burlington Magazine, CV, 1963, p8. He may also have used this collage technique in the 1527 More Family Group, S. Morison and N. Barker, The Likeness of Thomas More, London, 1963, pp27-28.

3 This information is derived from a scientific report by Miss Joyce Plesters of the National Gallery Scientific Department made when the Cartoon was acquired in 1957.

4 On which see E. Borsook, The Mural Painters of Tuscany, London, 1960, pp21 ff.

5 The Holbein copies of Henry VII and Elizabeth of York are very early, preceding in date most of the surviving examples which are, for the most part, Elizabethan or Jacobean. Versions of the Henry VII are at Helmingham Hall (Lord Tollemache), Society of Antiquaries (three), Christ Church, Oxford, Windsor Castle (HM The Queen) and elsewhere. Versions of the Elizabeth are listed by Millar, Catalogue, I, p52 (17).

6 W. A. Shaw, Three Inventories, p33.

7 Ibid., loc. cit, This was first suggested by Chamberlain, Holbein, II, p109. The connexion still seems to me to be tenable although rejected by H. A. Schmidt, Holbein, II, pp372ff. and F. Grossman, Holbein Studies–I Burlington Magazine, XCIII, 1951. pp40-43.

8 K. Parker, Holbein Drawings at Windsor Castle, London, 1945, p47 (39).

9 Chapuys to Antoine Perrenot May 18th, 1536, Letters and Papers, 1536, p374

Plate 30 Hans Holbein
Queen Jane Seymour
$19\frac{3}{4} \times 11\frac{1}{4}$ inches
Reproduced by gracious permission of
Her Majesty the Queen

Plate 29 Hans Holbein *Henry VIII*
$11 \times 7\frac{1}{2}$ inches
The Thyssen-Bornemisza Collection
Lugano

Plate 31   Hans Holbein *Queen Jane Seymour*
$25\frac{1}{2} \times 16$ inches
Kunsthistoriches Museum, Vienna

Plate 32   Hans Holbein *Queen Jane Seymour*
$10\frac{3}{8} \times 7\frac{3}{8}$ inches
Mauritshuis, The Hague

frontal face-mask was utilised yet again for Holbein's final unfinished picture of Henry VIII
and the Barber-Surgeons [Plate 34].[1]

The bulky figure of the King, legs astride, feet firmly planted on the ground, a fantastic
amalgam of the static and the swaggering, is accepted as Holbein's most definitive portrait
creation. No one ever thinks of Henry VIII in any other way than as this gouty, pig-eyed,
pile of flesh, whose astounding girth is only emphasised by the layers of slashed velvets and
furs that encase him. The alteration to the position of the head, in the Cartoon turned
slightly to the right glancing towards Queen Jane, to a frontal axis, was perhaps Holbein's
master touch. Henry alone communicates with the onlooker and the effect on visitors to
the palace was such that they 'were abashed, annihilated' in his presence.[2] The pose is
primarily one of latent energy, of as yet unleashed passion, again thrown brilliantly into
relief by the passive calm of the other three figures: the timidity of Queen Jane, her hands
clasped before her, the heavy-lidded langour of Henry VII and the static calm of his Queen.

1 R. Strong, *Holbein's Cartoon*, p11. I do not
accept Ganz's attribution of the Castle
Howard portrait, *Holbein*, plate 158.

2 C. van Mander, *Livre des Peintres*,
trans. H. Hymans, Paris, 1884, I, p218. This
presumably, but not certainly, refers to the
lost wall-painting. Van Mander would have
derived his information from his master, Lucas
de Heere, who was in England *circa* 1567 to
1576.

Plate 33 *Henry VIII*
Detail from the Chatsworth Cartoon

Plate 35 *Henry VIII* Detail from Plate 26

Plate 34 *Henry VIII* Detail from the Cartoon, *Henry VIII and the Barber-Surgeons*
Royal College of Surgeons Infra-red photograph

Plate 36   Donatello *St George*
Marble Height 6 feet 10 inches
Or San Michele, Florence

Plate 37   Perugino *St Michael*
50 × 25½ inches National Gallery, London

1 C. Gould, *An Introduction to Italian Renaissance Painting* London, 1962, p19. He discusses the dissemination of the pose but does not link it to the Holbein image.

The pose of Henry stems directly from a favourite formula for the heroic evolved in 15th century Florence. It can be traced back to Donatello's *St George* [Plate 36], executed about 1420 for the exterior of Or San Michele, and can be followed down through Andrea del Castagno's *Pippo Spano* in S. Apollonia, to Polliainolo's *David* and Perugino's *St Michael* [Plate 37].[1] All these figures are ones of knightly triumph against tremendous, often super-natural, powers. Henry VIII joins them in the double role of *imperator* and *chevalier*.

42

Plate 38   After Hans Holbein *Henry VIII*
92 × 53 inches Walker Art Gallery, Liverpool

Plate 39   William Scrots *Edward VI*
$65\frac{3}{4} \times 35\frac{3}{4}$ inches Reproduced by gracious permission of
Her Majesty the Queen

Plate 40   Robert Peake the Elder *Henry Prince of Wales à la chasse*
$79\frac{1}{2} \times 58$ inches Metropolitan Museum of Art, New York
Purchase 1944, Joseph Pulitzer Bequest

1 The most important early copies are (i) By
Hans Eworth, 1567, Trinity College, Cambridge,
J. W. Goodison, *Connoisseur*, CXXXIX, 1957,
p215 (5) rep.; (ii) Undated but also attributable
to Hans Eworth, Duke of Devonshire,
Chatsworth, L. Cust, *On the Portraits of Henry
VIII*, Burlington Magazine, XXXI, 1917,
p222 rep.; (iii) Undated but certainly mid-16th
century and probably the earliest copy, the
Walker Art Gallery, Liverpool (ex. East Knoyle)
(Plate 38). *Connoisseur*, CXV, 1945, p65 rep.

With this image of Henry VIII, the use of royal portraiture in England as propaganda in the modern sense of the word begins. The existence of so many copies and derivatives corroborates that this must have been looked upon as a portrait pattern to be multiplied. Three full length versions, all 16th century in date, are of immense importance in conveying to us something of the impact of the original [Plate 38].[1] Its effect on the iconography of his heir, the child-King, Edward VI, was decisive. Both the full length at Petworth, dated 1547, and the later full lengths by William Scrots [Plate 39],[2] follow the Holbein canon, although in the case of the latter it is poured into a mannerist mould. The reign of the two Queens who followed broke the tradition and it was not revived again for the official portraiture of the new dynasty. Peake's portrait of the heir apparent, Prince Henry *à la*

Plate 41   Bernardo Prevedari after Bramante *Architectural Fantasy*
Engraving

Continuing notes 1 & 2 from p. 44.
Other full length copies seem later, e.g. formerly in the collection of Lord Brocket (ex. Ditchley coll.), Belvoir Castle (Duke of Rutland), Petworth (Lord Egremont), and in the Parham Park Collection. The Petworth version (colour frontispiece) seems to be a copy direct from the wall painting itself before it was destroyed. It brings out particularly well the lavish use of gold on the architectural features.

2 On which see E. Auerbach, *Notes on Some Northern Mannerist Portraits*, Burlington Magazine, XCI, 1949, pp218-222. The threequarter length at Windsor may once have been a whole length in which case it would have been the earliest instance of the use of the Holbein formula for the heir to the throne see O. Millar, *Catalogue*, I, p64 (44), II, plate 21.

chasse [Plate 40], contains perhaps the last direct reference to this legendary formula for English royalty.

The carpet upon which the royal family stands contains a border of a pattern which recurs in a number of Holbein pictures,[1] and for the background the echoes of early Italian renaissance architecture are both confused and strong. In all probability it was designed both from memories of things seen on his Italian trip together with more tangible sources in the form of engravings. One by Bernardo Prevedari after an architectural fantasy by Bramante [Plate 41] has a number of features in common with the backcloth to the Privy Chamber group, not only the ubiquitous shell niches and pilasters but more particularly a great central arch encompassing a laurel garland roundel through which the back view of a

1 R. Strong, *Holbein's Cartoon*, p7, note 20.

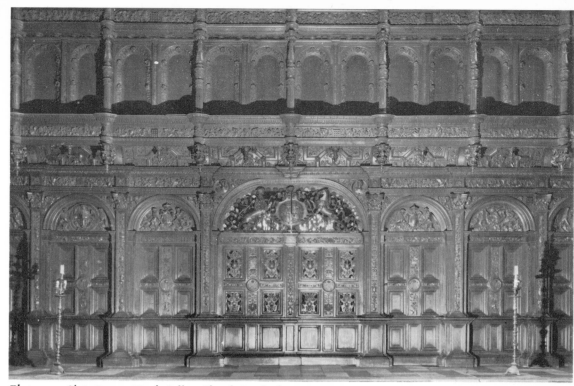

Plate 42   *Choir Screen, King's College Chapel, Cambridge*

1 A. M. Hind, *Early Italian Engraving*, London, 1948, V, Catalogue, plate 2, p102. This was first pointed out by Dr. Peter Murray. Schmidt's hypothesis (I, p84) of the renewed contact with Italian art circa 1531 is supported by Grossman (*Holbein Studies*–I, p40, and the same author in Journal of the Warburg and Courtauld Institutes, XIII, 1950, p233). As there is no historical evidence but merely deduced on grounds of style it seems to me to remain unproven. In respect of the Privy Chamber Group renewed contact is hardly evident.

2 A. M. Hind, op. cit, p23 (15b), plate 512. See also plate 593 Shell niches appear, for instance, on plate 664, 667.

3 This relationship of Holbein to other Italians in Henry VIII's service is discussed in A. E. Popham, 'Hans Holbein's Italian contemporaries in England' *Burlington Magazine* LXXXIV, 1944 pp. 12–17

classical bust can be seen.[1] Pilasters of the Privy Chamber type figure too at the end of the great series of engravings after Andrea Mantegna's Triumphs, a source used by Holbein for his own Triumphs of Riches and Poverty.[2] Italian carvers in the service of Henry VIII were in any case erecting in England this very type of architectural decoration[3]. The arches, pilasters and frieze in the wall-painting are but variations in paint of, for example, the choir-screen in King's College Chapel, Cambridge [Plate 42] erected by royal craftsmen in the years immediately preceding the Privy Chamber decoration. Indeed the chapel choir screen may accurately reflect of the type of panelling and carved decoration within Whitehall Palace itself.

It is indeed difficult to consider how Holbein could have carried through the Privy Chamber fresco without first-hand knowledge of the work of Mantegna. He was certainly familiar with and must have collected his engravings. Between the outspread legs of the

Plate 43   Hans Holbein *Enraged Warrior* Detail from Plate 1

King a relief can be seen depicting a male nude convulsed with rage, posed in an attitude of imminent attack, his left arm extended thrusting forward a shield, his right flung back menacing a bunch of dead fishes [Plate 43]. The quotation here could hardly be more direct and comes from Mantegna's engraving of the *Battle of the Sea Gods* [Plate 44]. Executed about 1490, it has been suggested that this stange composition derives from the account of the Icthyophagi in Diodorus Siculus as translated by Poggio Bracciolini.[1] For the most part Holbein had adapted the figure of the enraged male nude charging through the waters astride a sea horse, although elements too stem from the hippocamp on the second right hand sheet of the engraving who bears a horse's skull shield in his hand. This reference reminds us that Holbein's concept of wall painting stems from a knowledge of Mantegna rather than Raphael, and that the Privy Chamber, had it survived, would be viewed today

1 Ibid., p15. See also H. Delaborde, *La Gravure en Italie avant Marc-Antoine*, Paris and London, n.d. p271 where he traces the antique source.

Plate 44 Andrea Mantegna *The Battle of the Sea Gods* Engraving

Plate 45   Hans Holbein *The Ambassadors* (reproduced in reverse)
82 × 82¼ inches   National Gallery, London

as the northern equivalent of the *camerapicta* at Mantua rather than the Vatican stanze.

The four figures are welded together into a compositional form about which Holbein clearly puzzled much. Four years before, in 1533, he had tackled it on a less monumental scale in the group portrait of Jean de Dinteville, Lord of Polissy, and George de Selve, Bishop of Lavour, in the famous picture known as *The Ambassadors*, now in the National Gallery [Plate 45]. These two men flank a two-tiered table in exactly the same way as Henry VII and Elizabeth of York stand on either side of the altar. Indeed, in the case of the Bishop, the gestures are absolutely identical, but in reverse, to those of Henry VII, one hand leaning clasping gloves, the other grasping the edge of his long robe. The Privy Chamber Group takes up and elaborates the problems and statements made in the Ambassadors in 1533 but it does so in such a way that the ultimate source of Holbein's composition is little concealed. Without doubt if we had to point to an immediate single compositional source it would be to the classic high renaissance formula for a Madonna and

Child enthroned within a room flanked by saints.[1] An altarpiece by Cosimo Rosselli is taken as a random instance [Plate 46]. By removing the Virgin and Child the group would be reduced to four figures placed in an ascending order on either side of a marble dais. The source for Holbein's great work could not be more succinctly demonstrated.

But the crucial problem of both compositions is the absence of a central focal point. In the Ambassadors this is solved, more or less satisfactorily, by the wonderful still-life of books and instruments alluding to the arts and sciences pursued by the sitters, but the dedicatory altar in the Privy Chamber Group seems a very unsatisfactory substitute. The fact that the inscription appears on the Royal Collection copy and Edward VI is inserted into the Petworth version argues that Leemput is making good what was a blank in the

1 This was first demonstrated by D. Piper, *Holbein the Younger in England,* Journal of the Royal Society of Arts, CXI, 1953, p74-5.

Plate 46   Cosimo Rosselli *Madonna enthroned with Saints*
78 × 68½ inches   Fitzwilliam Museum, Cambridge

composition formed by some architectural feature of the room. At this point we should turn to the important, if highly unsatisfactory, evidence, provided by a French visitor to the Privy Chamber in 1671. He writes:

'In the antechamber of the King, there is on the gable of the window (sur le pignon de la croisée) by Holbein's hand, the portrait of Henry VIII, and the princes, his children . . .'[1]

Patin is clear on one point, the painting was around a window and this must have occupied the space where Leemput substituted the stone altar. He is wrong as to subject matter and his allusion to it being *sur le pignon* is the most cryptic of all. 'Pignon' in this sense means gable, the triangular upper feature of a house, and Cotgrave provides the meaning as it was understood in 1611: 'A Finiall, Cop, or small Pinacle on the ridge or top of a house'.[2] It is clear from this that the fresco was high up but it is impossible to reconcile what we know of it with anything triangular in shape. One can infer from it, however, that he meant that the painting covered the upper wall of the end of a room and that it encompassed a clerestory window.[3]

From what we know of early Tudor palace décor this is exactly what we should expect, the division of the walls of the room into two levels, a lower of panelling and an upper of plasterwork or painting. Above that would follow a freize and finally a richly pendented or compartmented ceiling. This is familiar both from Wolsey's closet at Hampton Court [Plate 47] and, perhaps, more particularly, from the drawing of 1543-47 for a throne room, which shows panelling with the badges of Katherine Parr below and complex plasterwork

1 C. Patin, *Relations Historiques*, Basle, 1673, pp211 ff.

2 R. Cotgrave, *A Dictionary of the French and English Tongues*. London, 1611.

3 To surround a window would be in accordance with standard renaissance practice in the same way as Raphael's *Parnassus* encompasses a door. Attempts to make croisée a misprint for cheminée seem pointless, Woltman, *Holbein*, p393.

Plate 47   *Wolsey's Closet, Hampton Court*

above in the manner of Fontainebleau [Plate 24].

In the light of this revelation we need to re-study the architecture which makes up the background of the Privy Chamber Group more closely.[1] Immediately it will be noticed that the architecture seems strangely independent of the group which floats out on a platform in front of it. There is no actual structural connexion between the two. Could it be that the niches, pilasters and frieze Holbein depicts in paint were in fact a continuation of the reality in plaster around the remainder of the upper part of the room? That this is a likely hypothesis can be inferred by reference back to an earlier comparable series of frescoes by Holbein, those in the Council Chamber at Basle. There he certainly fused the architecture of the room into the projections beyond it created in paint.[2] What, however, seems to prove the point beyond doubt is the mermen and mermaid frieze. A frieze almost identical with this in fact appears in Wolsey's Closet, admittedly less sophisticated but nonetheless basically the same [Plate 48]. What is more to the point, a frieze of this sort also appears in Holbein's own woodcut of the King enthroned in counsel [Plate 49] in a room which might almost be one in Whitehall Palace in the 1530's. Once we begin to visualise a room with an upper and lower storey the whole Privy Chamber fresco begins to be explicable in terms of Tudor Palace decoration and in terms of its own perspective which is that of an altarpiece, to which people gazed up.

1 On the role of illusory architecture in renaissance wall painting see A. Blunt, *Illusionist Decoration in Central Italian Painting of the Renaissance*, Journal of the Society of Arts, CVII, 1959, pp309-25; I. Bergström, *Revival of antique illusionistic wall-painting in Renaissance art*, Goteborgs Universitats Arsskrit, LXIII, 1957, pp27 ff; J. Schulz, *Pintoricchio and the Revival of Antiquity*, Journal of the Warburg and Courtauld Institutes, XXV, 1962, pp35-55; K. Simon, *The Dais and the Arcade: Architecture and Pictorial Narrative in quattrocento painting*, Apollo, LXXXI, 1965, pp270-78.

2 See P. Ganz, *Holbein*, figs 46-49. It would take us too far from the scope of this study to embark on a discussion of all Holbein's previous monumental commissions.

Plate 48   Artist unknown *Section of frieze from Wolsey's Closet*

Plate 49   Jacob Faber after Hans Holbein *Henry VIII in Council*
Wood engraving from Hall's *Chronicle* 1548

This integration of paint and plaster into one overall illusory effect is reflected in Holbein's choice of medium. The two other monumental commissions he executed earlier in England, the More Family Group of the first visit and the Triumphs of Riches and Poverty for the hall of the German Steelyard Merchants, had been detachable paintings let into their surroundings executed in some form of oil and tempera on linen. By the middle of the 17th century the More Family Group had already suffered much – it is described as *alquanto rovinato*.[1] But the link of the Tudor Family Group and its architectural setting was so strong that Holbein carried it out directly onto the surface of the wall itself. William

1 S. Morison and N. Barker, *More*, p20.

Plate 50 (a)   *Diagram showing the area covered by the cartoon:*
Plate 26 with Plate 1 superimposed

Plate 50 (b)   *Conjectured reconstruction of the Whitehall Privy Chamber* (Colin Sorensen)

53

Sanderson in his *Graphice* (1658), after lamenting the havoc wrought by damp on wall-paintings, goes on to refer to that 'excellent painting' carried out in 'Oyle only' which had 'been preserved with continuall warmth within doors, and benefit of fire, even till now. But withall; I observe the Wall, prim'd with a very thick Compost of Playster, and some other mixture fixed, to preserve the work'.[1] Clearly there was some layer of composition which insulated that bearing the paint layers.

But we are still left with a crucial problem, for the window admittedly solves the extra-ordinary appearance of the stone altar but it does not eliminate the fact that the composition still has no focal point. At this juncture we should return to the room and its use, for as the principal reception and living room of the private apartments it could, therefore, only have one possible axis: the King himself. This in turn brings us to the position of the dais, chair and cloth of estate.[2] No one will probably ever know the exact lay-out of the room but surely there could only ever have been one place possible for it, that is beneath the great wall painting itself, the King transforming into actuality the world of paint above him. In order to complete Holbein's painting we should visualise the gross figure of Henry VIII, supreme head next to Christ of the church in England, enthroned beneath, the living embodiment of the genealogy of the Houses of York and Lancaster above him [Plate 50b]. Framed by such a setting the King is seen, in the words of Hall, his chronicler, as 'the indubitate flower, and very heir of both the sayd lineages'.

1 N. Sanderson, *Graphice*, p24.

2 We know there was a cloth of estate in the Privy Chamber. One of the specific tasks of the Gentleman Usher under Edward VI was to keep this in order: *Antiquarian Repertory*, London, 1809, IV, pp648-53. During a Privy Chamber reception of 1595, Queen Elizabeth I is referred to as having greeted an envoy and 'then turned back and seated herself upon a chair under a canopy of cloth and gold', Von Klarwill, *Queen Elizabeth and Some Foreigners*, p363.

Plate 51   Unknown artist *Philip and Mary enthroned, beneath a canopy with windows above* Illuminated Plea Roll initial, Michaelmas 1554 Public Record Office

THE INDUBITATE FLOWER

The Rose both White and Red
*   In one Rose now doth grow:*
Thus through every sted
*   Thereof the fame doth blow.*
*   Grace the seed did sow:*
England, now gather floures,
Exclude now all doloures.

Noble Henry the Eight,
*   They loving sovereign lord,*
Of kinges line most straight
*   His title doth well accord*
Alexis young of age,
Adrastus wise and sage,

Astrea, Justice hight,
*   That from the Starry sky*
Shall now come and do right.
*   This hundred year scantly*
*   A man could not espy*
That Right dwelt us among,
And that was the more wrong.

John Skelton,
A Laud and Praise made for
our Sovereign Lord the King[1]

[1] *The Complete Poems of John Skelton*, ed.
P. Henderson, London and Toronto, 1931, p25.

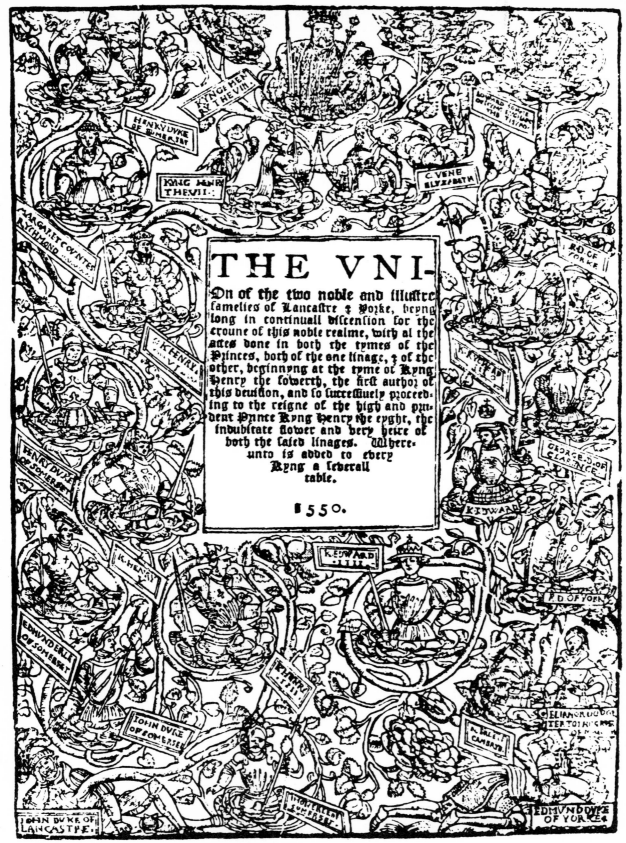

Plate 52   Artist unknown *Rose Tree of the House of Tudor*
Woodcut from Hall's *Chronicle* 1550

The existence of a window occupying the place transformed by Leemput into a stone altar leaves us to account for the Latin verses which appear on the Royal Collection version. They read as follows:

SI IVVAT HEROVM CLARAS VIDESSE FIGURAS,
    SPECTA HAS, MAIORES NVLLA TABELLA TVLIT.
CERTAMEN MAGNVM, LIS, QVAESTIO MAGNA PATERNE.
    FILIVS AN VINCAT. VICIT. VTERQVE QVIDEM.
ISTE SVOS HOSTES, PATRIAEQVE INCENDIA SAEPE
    SVSTULIT, ET PACEM CIVIBVS VSQUE DEDIT.

FILIVS AD MAIORA QVIDEM PROGNATVS AB ARIS
    SVBMOVET INDIGNOSI SVBSTITVITQVE PROBOS.
CERTAE, VIRTVTI, PAPARVM AVDACIA CESSIT,
    HENRICO OCTAVO SCEPTRA GERENTE MANV
REDDITA RELIGIO EST, ISTO REGNANTE DEIQVE
    DOGMATA CEPERVNT ESSE IN HONORE SVO.

Or, in translation:

If it rejoice thee to behold the glorious likenesses of heroes, look on these, for greater no tablet ever bore. Great the contest (and) the rivalry, great the debate whether the father or the son were victor. Each was the victor, the father over his foes, for he quenched the fires of civil strife and to his people granted lasting peace.

The son, born to yet greater destiny, from the altars banished the undeserving and in their place set men of worth. To his outstanding virtue the presumption of popes yielded, and when Henry VIII in his hand wielded the sceptre (true) religion was restored, and in his reign the precepts of God began to be held in their due honour.[1]

1 I am much indebted to Miss Margot Eates for providing a new translation of the verses.

On the surface these verses capture so well the mood of the wall painting that one would be tempted to believe that they formed part of the original Privy Chamber schema. In this,

1 Information kindly given by Mr. Ronald Lightbown.

2 The Union of the Roses surpassed all other early Tudor themes of dynastic glorification. See S. Anglo, *The British History in Early Tudor Propaganda*, Bulletin of the John Rylands Library, XLIV, 1961-62, pp17-48 for a reassessment of the use of Arthurianism.

3 *Anglica Historia*, ed. Hay ppxxiii ff.

4 Ibid., pxxviii.

5 *Anglica Historia*, ed. Hay, p149.

however, we would be wrong for the relationship of the verses to the little Leemput copy alone is proved by the use of the word *tabella,* which cannot refer to a wall painting.[1] Nonetheless we should not discard the verses altogether for they tell us what people thought the Privy Chamber painting was about in 1667.

The composition is more particularly a statement in paint of the official Tudor view of English History, of peace engendered through the fruitful union of rival dynastic houses.[2] Examining such a monumental composition so charged with historical associations, it is difficult mentally to discard all events after 1537. In that year the Tudors had completed fifty-two years of rule from that day in August 1485 when Henry Tudor was acclaimed King on Bosworth Field. The consolidation of the dynasty was a lengthy process stretching through Henry VII's reign down until 1541, when the final Plantagenet, Margaret Pole, Countess of Salisbury, was butchered on a charge of conspiracy. Even then, the hopes of the Catholic powers centred on her son, Reginald, Cardinal Pole. The Tudors were throughout their rule faced with rival claimants to the throne and by a succession of attempts by means of rebellion or assassination to disrupt their rule. In addition, after the reign of Henry VIII, the descent of the Crown was a less clear cut issue. All this explains the relentless concern with succession in their propaganda: they had to be presented, by divine right as it were, as the pre-ordained rulers of England.

In relation to the Holbein wall painting, we can follow it in a number of ways in the reigns of Henry VII and Henry VIII. The accession of the Tudors coincided with a revolution in historical method and Henry VII was quick to bring into the service of the Crown the historiographical techniques of renaissance humanism. These were embodied above all in the *Anglica Historia* of Polydore Vergil, the importance of whose work in establishing the myth of empire we have already touched upon. As against the medieval schema of human history being written within the framework of divine revelation, the humanists, inspired by the writings of the historians of antiquity, saw history as a pageant of heroes.[3] 'It displays', writes Vergil in his dedication to Henry VIII, 'eternally to the living those events which should be an example and those which should be a warning'.[4] A distaste for monastic chronicles and scorn for the fabulous went hand in hand with the belief that history should be an argument and in this case it centred on the descent of the *imperium* to the House of Tudor. The theme of the whole saga may be summed up by the opening passage to his account of Henry VIII's reign:

'In earlier books we have explained . . . how King Richard II entirely lacked male heirs, and how not long after the whole population of England was split into two factions, Lancastrian and Yorkist, and how a bloody struggle ensued for over a hundred years, indeed until our own day, till at last the houses of Lancaster and York were united. The fruit of this union was Henry, in whom the true royal lines were joined. . . . I have now come to an end of my writing at a fortunate time; for I, who previously in describing party strife dwelt for long on the cruel slaughter of civil war, now – all faction dead – come to the description of a most quiet and flourishing condition of the state'.[5]

It is as though the whole of English history were but a prologue for the age of the Tudors, an inevitable progression towards a golden age. Indeed, Vergil views the match of Henry VII and Elizabeth of York as *divinitus factum:*

'He then took in marriage Elizabeth, daughter of Edward, a woman indeed intelligent above all others, and equally beautiful. It is legitimate to attribute this to divine intervention, for plainly by it all things which nourished the two most ruinous factions were utterly removed, by it the two houses of York and Lancaster were united and from the union the true and established royal line emerged which now reigns'.[1]

1 Ibid., p7.

We can catch the myth of Union in the making also in the hands of the court poets. Petrus Carmelianus' poem on the birth of Prince Arthur, *Laetitiae ad Angliam*, is typical of a number of poems, productions by the Latin humanist poets surrounding Henry VII glorifying the Tudors.[2] Carmelianus narrates how God, having compassion on the cruel strife rending the Kingdom of England, convokes a meeting of the saints, who advise an appeal to King Henry VI. The martyr King sees a solution in Union. Edward IV being dead, the crown has been usurped by his brother, who has treacherously murdered the true heirs, just as he had dealt the fatal blow to Henry VI himself. But Edward IV's eldest daughter Elizabeth, *pulcherrima virgo*, yet lives, as indeed does the heir of Lancaster, Henry of Richmond. After the defeat of the tyrant Richard, their marriage binds the rival houses and in their eldest child, Arthur, the blood of both York and Lancaster mingles:

2 See *Memorials of King Henry VII*, ed. J. Gairdner, London, 1858, Rolls series, ppliv-lxii. He cites also John de Giglis's *Epithalamium*, (B. M. Harleian MS 336) on the marriage. See also the draft for an oration to the Pope on the occasion of the marriage (B. M. Cotton MS Cleopatra E. III.f.123) in *Letters and Papers illustrative of the Reigns of Richard III and Henry VII*, ed. J. Gairdner, London, 1851, Rolls series, I, p421. See also S. Anglo, *The Foundation of the Tudor Dynasty*, Guildhall Miscellany, II, no 1, 1960, pp10-11.

'... nascitur ecce puer.
Nascitur ecce puer quo non generosior alter,
    Seu matrem quaeras, seu magis ipse patrem.
Nascitur ecce puer gemino de sanguine regum,
    Firma salvs regni perpetuumque decus'.[3]

3 *Memorials*, op. cit, plviii.

The most popular and most widely influential version of the Tudor myth was Hall's Chronicle first published in 1548. The full title sums up his argument: *The Vnion of the two noble and illustre fameles of Lancastre and Yorke, beeyng long in continual discension for the croune of this noble realme, with all the actes done in bothe the tymes of the Princes, bothe of the one linage, & of the other, beginnyng at the tyme of King Henry the fowerth, the first aucther of this deuision, and so successiuely proceeding to the reigne of the high and prudent Prince Kynge Henry the eight, the undubitate flower and very heire of both the saied linages'.* Hall's history is a saga moving dramatically from concord to discord and back to harmony again.[4] Like Vergil, he reaches a climax with the reign of Henry VIII and each reign is given its own particular character: the 'unquiet time' of Henry IV, the 'victorious actes' of Henry V, the 'troubleous season' of Henry VI, the 'prosperous reigne' of Edward IV, the 'pitiful life' of Edward V, the 'tragicall doinges' of Richard III, the 'politic gouernauce' of Henry VII and lastly the 'triumphant reigne' of Henry VIII. The story is found in visual form on the frontispiece to the 1550 edition where two great rose trees arise from the sleeping figures of John, Duke of Lancaster, and Edmund, Duke of York, bearing in their branches the chief exponents of the rival houses. [Plate 51] At the top where Henry VII and Elizabeth of York extend and join hands, two branches sprout from them supporting a large Tudor rose in which sits a gargantuan Henry VIII flanked by two more roses. The theme of the frontispiece is a less sophisticated version of the theme of the Holbein wall painting and the connexion between the form of the genealogical tree and the genesis of the first royal family portrait group is compelling. Hall's passage on the marriage of Henry and Elizabeth reads like a scheme for the painting:

4 *Anglica Historia*, ed. Hay, ppxxxvi-xxxvii.

1 E. Hall, *The Vnion of the Two Noble and Illustre Famelies of Lancastre and Yorke*, London, 1809, pp424-25.

'By reason of whiche mariage peace was thought to discende oute of heaven into England, consideryng that the lynes of Lancastre & Yorke, beyng both noble famylies equivalent in ryches, fame and honoure, were now brought into one knott and connexed together, of whose two bodyes one heyre might succede, which after their tyme should peaceably rule and enioye the whole monarchy and realme of England'.[1]

1537
A YEAR OF TRIUMPH

'And forasmuche as by th'inestimable goodnes and grace of Almighty God we be delivred and brought in child bed of a Prince . . . we have thought good to certifie youe of the same. To th'intent ye might not only rendre unto God condigne thankes and praise for soo greate a benefite, but alsoo continually pray for the long continuance and preservacion of the same here in this lief . . .'

Letter of Jane Seymour, 12th October, 1537[1]

[1]*The Literary Remains of King Edward VI*, ed. J. G. Nichols, Roxburghe Club, 1847, I, pxxiii.

Plate 53   Detail of frieze from Plate 1

The cartouches supported by mermen and mermaid that appear over the heads of Henry and his Queen in the Cartoon bear their initials, H and J intertwined by true lovers knots, but according to the Leemput copy the cartouches finally carried the date: ANNO 1537. That is, we are given a definite point in time, the year 1537, and by the year 1537 we mean the year as it was understood by the Tudors, running from March 25th 1537 to March 24th 1537/8. During this period one more of the sitters died, for on October 24th, Jane Seymour passed away, twelve days after she had given birth to an infant prince, the future Edward VI. The painting is, therefore, much more than a monument to the past, a reminder to the living of former glories, it is part of the fabric of the present, here, now, at this very moment in the year of Our Lord 1537.

Whitehall Palace was virtually complete in time to receive Henry's second Queen after her coronation so that the Privy Chamber Group was clearly never part of the *mise-en-scène* as it was originally conceived. This throws the wall painting even more sharply into the present, for it must have been deliberately commissioned by the King, a major addition to the already sumptuous interior of the palace. It belongs to the political mood of the moment and as it began at the opening of the year 1537 in April this was one of shattering victory for the Tudor dynasty. At home a major uprising in favour of the old order and the old ways of life had been defeated. Abroad the King of France and the Emperor had declined to lift a finger to implement the Pope's appeal to dethrone the tyrant. The papal legate, Cardinal Pole, had fled in confusion to Liège at the disastrous drift of events. In short, Henry VIII had emerged triumphant from the greatest single crisis of his reign: the Pilgrimage of Grace.[1]

The winter of 1536-37 had indeed been one of turbulence and unrest. It began in November in Lincolnshire. In that county the implementation of the suppression of the lesser monastic houses coincided with the collection of the subsidy. On October 1st and 2nd there were risings at Louth and Caister, evoked by the arrival of the King's Visitors bent on the dissolution of the local houses. In no time whole villages rose in protest and local gentry families were forced to join the revolt which spread in a matter of days through the whole county. They demanded the restoration of the religious houses, a remission of the subsidy, an abolition of the payment of First Fruits and Tenths to the Crown, the repeal of the Statute of Uses, the elimination of councillors of base blood from the King's table and the removal of heretical bishops. Lord Hussey of Sleaford, conservative at heart, made no attempt to stem the tide of rebellion. Meanwhile, an army was raised in the south to march on the Lincolnshire rebels. At its approach the insurgents fell out amongst themselves, the gentry

1 The following account of the events of 1536-37 is based on M. H. and R. Dodds, *The Pilgrimage of Grace and the Exeter Conspiracy,* Cambridge U.P, 1915, 2 vols; Introduction to *Letters and Papers,* 1536 and 1537 vols; J. A. Froude, *History of England,* London, n.d, II and III.

going over to the King, with the result that the Duke of Suffolk and the other royalist commanders entered Lincoln as conquerors. The rebellion in Lincolnshire had no sooner started than it was over. The King did not mince matters in his message to the rebels: 'How presumptuous, then, are ye, the rude commons of one shire, and that one of the most brute and beastly of the whole realm, and of least experience, to take upon you, contrary to God's law and man's law, to rule your prince whom ye are bound to obey and serve, and for no worldly cause to withstand?'

The unrest in Lincolnshire was but a rehearsal for further blows to come, for the second week in October saw outbreaks of revolt in all the northern towns, a movement of dissatisfaction with the central government which coalesced under the leadership of one man, a London barrister, Robert Aske. As in Lincolnshire, the rapidity with which it spread owed much to the inaction of a conservative peer, this time Lord Darcy. On October 14th, the rebels camped on Weighton Common under Aske and the day after marched on York which opened its gates. Lord Darcy meanwhile prevaricated under siege, together with the Archbishop of York, in Pomfret Castle. On the 20th, this fell to the rebels and Lord Darcy and the rest of its distinguished inmates were sworn to the cause of the insurgents. By the close of October almost all the great northern families had declared for the rebels who marched south to Doncaster to meet the advancing royalist army. The demands of those who led the Pilgrimage of Grace were similar to those of Lincolnshire: they included the restoration of papal power, the suppression of heresy, the legitimisation of the Princess Mary, the restoration of the abbeys, the abolition of First Fruits and Tenths, the summoning of a northern parliament and the inevitable removal of the base blood of Cromwell, Rich and the rest of them from the King's Council table. The movement was so strong and the numbers so overwhelming that the leader of the royalist army, Norfolk, was forced to parley. Lords Latimer, Lumley, Darcy, Sir Robert Constable, and Sir John Bulmer met an equal number of knights and noblemen from Norfolk's army. An armistice was declared while their petition was borne to the King. Henry played for time, knowing that a split between the 'gentles' and 'rude rusticalles' was inevitable. The weeks dragged by and the forces of rebellion were assailed internally, as was anticipated, by division. Then, at last, early in December, the King's concessions to the pilgrims arrived and Norfolk, by clever stage-management, seemed to promise all in the King's name. They either believed, or were left with the impression, that Henry had given in to their demands. Aske promptly pulled off his pilgrim's badge, bearing the five wounds of Christ, and swore 'We will wear no badge nor figure but the badge of our sovereign Lord'.

The settlement at Doncaster was a pyrrhic victory depending entirely on the word of the King and the goodwill of his government. Both were determined to lay low the north at the earliest possible opportunity. Large garrisons were thrown into Newcastle, Scarborough and Hull and when Sir Francis Bigod of Mogreve Castle sent up the alarm that all the hopes of the rebels had been betrayed, the government found its justification to strike. The renewed outbreaks of disorder were repaid by rapid and ruthless suppression by the Duke of Norfolk acting on Henry's instructions: 'our pleasure is . . . you shall cause such dreadful execution to be done upon a good number of the inhabitants of every town, village and hamlet that have offended, as they may be a fearful spectacle to all others hereafter that would practise any like matter'. The pilgrims' lot was hardly ameliorated by the arrival of the papal legate, Reginald Pole, created Cardinal for this very mission. Simultaneously with his appearance at Cambray, Robert Aske, Lord Darcy and Sir Robert Constable were arrested and sent to the Tower. A leader of the Lincolnshire rebels was hanged on March 8th and twelve more ended on gibbets up and down the county. The fate of the various northern rebels was more complex in its stage-management. Lord Darcy was executed on Tower Hill on June 20th. Bigod, the Abbots of Fountains and Jervaulx, Sir John Bulmer and others were hanged at Tyburn. On Friday in Whitsun week Lady Bulmer was dragged through the streets to be burnt at the stake. Lord Hussey was executed at Lincoln, Constable was hanged in chains at Hull and Robert Aske at York. Amidst a welter of bloody savagery the Pilgrimage of Grace came to its end.

But all was mirth and revelry at court during the late spring and summer of 1537 for the Queen, Jane Seymour, was pregnant. On Trinity Sunday, May 27th, a solemn Te Deum was ordered to be sung in St Paul's and orders were given for York and Calais to follow suit. At last, five months later 'In Octobre on saynct Edwardes even was borne at Hampton court the noble Impe Prince Edward . . . At the byrth of this noble Prince was great fyers made through the whole realme and great Joye made wyth thankesgeving to almightie God, which had sent so noble a prince to succede in the croune of this realme'.[1] Even though the child's birth was overshadowed twelve days later by the death of his mother, the rejoicings were widespread and spontaneous. Now at last the procession of events over the last few years, from the first mooting of the King's Great Matter, bore fruit in a male heir of the blood royal whose succession to the imperial diadem of the kingdom should ensure the continuance of the Tudor pax.

The theme of the wall painting is one of victory and fruition. The Pilgrims, 'the rebellious Guarryson of Satan' of the royalist narratives, were crushed. They who had decked themselves out in 'false and counterfeated signes of holynes . . . only to delude and decyue the symple and ignorant people' had reaped the bloody reward due to men who date lift a hand against God's earthly viceregent.[2] Henry bestrides the scene as 'an Arke of all princely goodnes and honour', a hero who was 'not onely the noblest kynge that euer reigned ouer the english nation, but also pater patriae, that is, the father of our countrey, one by whose vertue, lernyng, and noble courage, England is neweborne, newly brought from thraldome to freedome'.[3]

1 *Henry VIII* by Edward Hall, ed. Whibley, II, p279.

2 This official view is given in two pamphlets by Sir Richard Morison, *A Lamentation in whiche is shewed what Ruyne and destruction cometh of seditious rebellyon*, London, 1536 and *A Remedy for Sedition*, London, 1536.

3 Henry Parker, Lord Morley, *The Exposition and declaration of the Psalme*, London 1534, dedication.

EPILOGUE

'*Yf your pleasure be to have the paterne of this here,
I knowe right wel the Frenche King woll geve
it me.*'

Sir John Wallop to Henry VIII on the gallery
at Fontainebleau, 17th November 1540[1]

---

[1] Sir John Wallop to Henry VIII, 17th November 1540, A. Chamberlain, *Holbein*, II, p333.

Plate 54   Attributed to Nicolò da Modena
Francis I as Minerva and other deities
Bibliothèque Nationale, Paris

1 O. Kurz, *An Architectural Design for Henry VIII*, Burlington Magazine, LXXXII, 1943, pp81-83.

2 D. and E. Panofsky, *The Iconography of the Galerie Francois Ier*, Gazette des Beaux Arts, LII, 1958, pp113 ff.

3 First exhibited in L'Europe Humaniste, Palais des Beaux-Arts, Bruxelles, 1954 (50). It was formerly attributed to Niccolo dell'Abbate but the alternative attribution to Modena seems perfectly reasonable, although it would have to be before 1538 in date.

There were no successors to the Privy Chamber décor and there was a very cogent reason for this. Holbein's painting represents the sole manifestation of high renaissance illusionistic wall painting in England as it was known in renaissance Italy. The contrast with the gay pageant frescoes of the Orchard Gallery of five years before could not have been more striking and places Holbein's masterpiece on the cool, classic heights of pure renaissance classicism, to that stream which runs direct from Mantegna and reaches fruition in Raphael's stanze. It stands alone embodying a brief fleeting moment in time. Already elsewhere that moment had passed and a new style was sweeping the courts of Europe, one which we term in modern art historical jargon, 'mannerism'.

Holbein's wall painting represents the Crown's earliest venture into the use of illusory room decoration and it may well have been prompted by news crossing the channel of the wonders of the new gallery being decorated by Rosso at Fontainebleau. Henry VIII, ever anxious to keep in line with the fashions set by the French court, was well aware of the glories of that palace. The year after Holbein had finished his painting, Henry began his breakneck building project of Nonsuch and the decoration of this was carried out under the auspices of one of the chief artists who had actually worked at Fontainebleau, Nicolò da Modena. We only have to glance at the design for a throne room [Plate 24], almost certainly by him, to realise that we are in a different world from that of Holbein[1]. Under Nicolò's auspices, the King's later palace decoration became a naturalisation of the stucco and paint formula first evolved in France by Primaticcio and Rosso in the early fifteen thirties. Nonsuch, had it survived, would have presented iconographers no doubt with major problems in the same way as scholars have puzzled over the abstruse layers of meaning to be extracted from Rosso's schema for the Galerie François Premier. There is moreover implicit in this technique a major revolution in the method of glorification which is, as Panofsky says, one by means of 'allusive correlation', a system depending upon the exact parallel of contemporary themes with those from the myths and legends of classical antiquity.[2] Nicolò da Modena's extraordinary portrait of Francis I as *Minerva* [Plate 54] epitomises the radical shift in the apparatus of apotheosis from the straightforward family group of Holbein.[3] In short, it was Nicolò da Modena and not Holbein who must have provided the court of Henry VIII in its final years with the perfect foil for its gaudy life. A complex of rich marquetry-work enhanced by friezes of sculpted figures and paintings, together with a profusion of detail and a swaying sinuosity of line must have made the staturesque family

Plate 55   Begun by Hans Holbein
Henry VIII and the Barber-Surgeons
63 × 110 inches   The Worshipful Company of Barbers

group by Holbein seem very dated almost as soon as it was finished. One remains astounded that in the decade 1530 to 1540 the early Tudor court had managed at whirlwind speed to run through the final phase of late medieval narrative painting, on through the quintessence of high renaissance illusionism, arriving finally at a riot of ebullient mannerism.

There is no evidence that Holbein was employed again by the Crown for interior decoration. Although in the estimation of the Court he was to remain supreme as a portraitist until his death, during the last five years of his life he was swiftly becoming old-fashioned, the living embodiment of an earlier era. His final great unfinished commission, the group portrait of Henry VIII and the Barber Surgeons, came not from the Crown but from a City Company [Plate 49]. Generations of scholars have commented upon its archaic quality and this is thrown dramatically into relief when it is set within the perspective of the new tastes of the Court. Holbein by the opening of the fifth decade of the sixteenth century must have seemed decidedly passé.

If we wish for further evidence of his archaism we have only to turn to any of the portraits produced during his second English period. It is all too easy to be overwhelmed by the brilliant virtuosity of technique, that coup d'oeil which marks his finest work, away from realising how old-fashioned his portraiture was. By the mid-thirties Titian had introduced a new sombre richness to portraiture, a new grand formal informality which entranced the Habsburg court and the Venetian aristocracy. During the same period Bronzino was evolving his pallid icons of the Medici court at Florence, turning away from the startling realism of early renaissance portraiture, of which Holbein was the prime exponent in the north, to the production of sumptuously upholstered wax dolls. In addition the props of portraiture had changed and the era of the satin curtain, the column and the distant landscape had arrived. In England Holbein's successor, William Scrots, was to embody this vapid sleekness in his portrait of Edward VI [Plate 39].

The Barber-Surgeons Group [Plate 49] does, however, have something to add to our story, for in it Holbein takes up and reaffirms for the last time the statements he made in the great Privy Chamber Group. The dedication inscribed on the cartouche glorifies Henry VIII as 'Defender of the Faith, and next to Christ, Supreme Head of the Church of England and Ireland'. Latin verses sing a paean of praise in honour of the King who has raised the enfeebled minds of his subjects by 'the light of the gospel', which now 'flies around on glowing wings'. The full frontal image is much more stiff and icon-like than that used on the earlier, woodcut, Bible frontispiece. He sits, his face composed into an expression of calm and never-ending vision, an image of *divina majestas,* the materialisation in paint of Bishop Gardiner's eulogy of him as 'the ymage of God vpon earthe'.[1]

Propaganda and great art are, of course, not incompatible and if we are to sum up Holbein's achievement during his last years in England it is this that we should bear in mind. Through him the new art forms were brought into the service of one of the new national monarchies. Subconsciously, or perhaps even deliberately, he transmutes the hallowed formulae of sacred art into tributes to a new and omnipotent monarchy which claims as the chief jewel in its Crown to be Vicar of Christ. Suppliants kneel imploring the protection not of Our Lady of Mercy but of the King; Henry, his Queen and parents pay homage not to the Virgin or to St George, but stand gazing outwards commanding homage to themselves as preservers of the Tudor pax and vanquishers of papal tyranny and impurity. It is not the Pope, nor the episcopacy, but the King who distributes the holy scriptures to awaiting bishops and laity. The English royal portrait as a means of propaganda is born with Holbein. The fact that we are unable to visualise Henry VIII in any other way except through the eyes of Holbein is evidence enough of his success as an official apologist.

Henry VIII outlived Holbein by four years and when death finally came it was at 'glorious Whyte Hall' on January 28th, 1547:

'Then was the Corps in the Chest had into the midst of his privy Chamber and set upon tressels with a rich pall of Cloath of gold and a Cross thereon, with all manner of lights thereto requisite, having divine service about him with Masses, obsequies and prayers, and continually watche being made by his Chapelrys Ordinary and Gentlemen of his Privy Chamber to the number of 30 persons'.[2]

Beneath Holbein's great masterpiece this turbulent King came to his rest.

1 This summarizes R. Strong, *Holbein's Cartoon.*

2 Quoted by E. Sheppard, *The Old Royal Palace of Westminster,* p292.

The early history of the Cartoon is unknown but as a working drawing it was presumably in the artist's possession and its descent seems likely to have been the same as that of the portrait drawings now at Windsor. These are assumed to have been acquired directly or indirectly by Henry FitzAlan, 17th Earl of Arundel (1512-1580), a man of considerable culture, whose two learned daughters married Thomas Howard, Duke of Norfolk, and John, Lord Lumley. Both daughters predeceased him. His links with his son-in-law, Lumley, were so close that he was Arundel's sole executor and residuary legatee. In addition, Lumley took over Nonsuch Palace (purchased by Arundel from Mary) where most of the collection was housed.

1590 First certain record in the inventory of pictures belonging to John, 1st Lord Lumley, drawn up in 1590 on the occasion of Nonsuch being returned to the Crown: 'The Statuary of King Henry the eight and his father Kinge Henry the seaventh joyned together, doone in white and blacke by Haunce Holbyn'. (Walpole Society, VI, 1918, p.21). Passed on Lumley's death in 1609 to his widow. Under her auspices most of the collection, including presumably the Cartoon, was transported to Lumley Castle which, on her death in 1617, passed to Richard Lumley, great-grandson of the 4th Lord Lumley. Richard was knighted in 1616 and created viscount in 1628 and his grandson became the 1st Earl of Scarbrough, in 1690. Although there were no public sales from the collection until 1780 it is clear that there were leakages before that date. At what date the cartoon left the Castle is not known.

1727 By 1727 the Cartoon had passed into the possession of William Cavendish, 2nd Duke of Devonshire:
'a drawing on paper. a Carton. Indian Ink. K.Hen. 7. K.Hen.8. by Holben. part of that design. (destroyd by the fire) at Whitehall. this being probably the pounce. for that picture, being prickt out line.
there is wanting the two Queens. the faces not finisht . . .' (*Notebooks*, Walpole Society II, p.36). See also for an almost identical note, *Notebooks*, VI, p.72.

1760 Seen by Horace Walpole on a visit to Chatsworth:
'Here is a large cartoon big as life & boldy drawn, of Henry 7th and 8th half of Holbein's original design for the great picture that was at Whitehall of those Kings & their Queens'. (Walpole Society, xvi, 1928, p.29).

1762 Recorded by Walpole in his *Anecdotes* when talking of the lost painting:
'Holbein's original drawing of the two kings is in the collection of the Duke of Devonshire. It is in black chalk, heightened, and large as life; now at Chatsworth. The architecture of this picture is very rich, and parts of it in a good style (*Anecdotes*, ed. Dallaway, London, 1862 ed., I, p.82).

Erratum: page 42 line 4 for Polliainolo read Pollaiuolo